TODAY'S
WOMAN:
IN SEARCH OF
Freedom

TODAY'S WOMAN: IN SEARCH OF Freedom

Ruthe White

HARVEST HOUSE PUBLISHERS
Eugene, Oregon 97402

Except where otherwise indicated, all Scripture quotations in this book are taken from The Living Bible, Copyright © 1971 by Tyndale House Publishers, Wheaton, Illinois. Used by permission.

Verses marked KJV are taken from the King James Version of the Bible.

TODAY'S WOMAN: IN SEARCH OF FREEDOM

Copyright © 1985 by Harvest House Publishers
Eugene, Oregon 97402

Library of Congress Catalog Card Number 85-60130
ISBN 0-89081-473-2

Printed in the United States of America.

To KEVIN and KOBY

With appreciation to Betsy Rogers, the typist,
who worked with me on this manuscript.

Contents

STEP II

DARE TO CHANGE

STEP III

COUNT THE COST

STEP IV

FREEDOM: IT'S WORTH IT!

- Do those who seek really find?
- What did Jesus mean when He said, "Come"?

Would you like to sponsor
a women's study group
using this book?

WRITE ME!

Ruthe White
P.O. Box 1346
Crestline, CA 92325

STEP I

MOMENT OF AWAKENING

. . . come, let us walk in the light of the Lord,
and be obedient to his laws!

Isaiah 2:5b

WHILE WE MAY NOT FULLY UNDERSTAND
THE MEANING OF FREEDOM, WE ALL SEEK IT.

Chapter 1

The Awareness
of Your Need

Because there is some person, thing, or circum-
stance in each of our lives from which we would like
to be free, our search for freedom becomes an
individual one. The awareness of a self-need is the
motivating force that propels us forward in that search
for personal freedom. The urgency of our need moves
us from where we presently are to where we want
to be.

We all know life rarely provides us all the advantages we seek. Since few of us, if any, have lived out
all the dreams that the "little girl" in us promised to
give, we are often disappointed in the women we
have become. We might even feel captive to the
society in which we live, angered by the lack of

so-called opportunities. This feeling of psychological bondage, along with our growing concern and search for fulfillment, touches every part of our lives. Our search for freedom drives us to seek careers, educational privileges, and the recognition of our rights as individuals. We are on a search!

Who are we?

We are women from all backgrounds, age groups, and environmental settings. We are persons inside the church and outside its membership. We have other roles as well. We are wives, mothers, employees, executives, and individuals who feel life. We hurt with our husbands, empathize with the needs of our children, and are an active part of our communities. We work hard on our jobs and in our homes. We seek creativity and long for a sense of belonging. We seek freedom—not only for ourselves, but for our children as well.

Which of us has never wished for a day free from responsibilities and the "dirty-dish" syndrome? We all have! The mother whose hours are filled with wiping noses, feeding hungry mouths, and washing loads of soiled laundry certainly has. The secretary, office manager, cosmetologist, or daily worker is often tempted to stop and ask herself: *Where has my freedom gone?*

You may be reading this and thinking: *But I enjoy my work, have no problems juggling roles, and am not a twentieth-century woman caught in a search for freedom.* If so, think with me for a moment:

There are many forms of bondage! Yours may be physical, psychological, and spiritual (whichever, the need is equally real). Perhaps you are struggling with the need for a personal kind of freedom. A broken relationship in your life may have you mentally and psychologically bound. A phobic reaction, superstition, feelings of guilt, or an unforgiving spirit may be holding you captive, while your spirit is yearning to find freedom. No matter what your need is, or the source from which it springs, there is freedom for you!

God understands. He never fragments our already-frail psyche. His only purpose in coming to us in our search is to put us back together after life has broken us into pieces. Matthew the apostle understood the principle to which I refer, for it was he who said of Jesus:

> He does not crush the weak, or quench
> the smallest hope" (Matthew 12:20).

Out of this context we come to God seeking a new beginning, healing for our broken dreams, fulfillment, and acceptance. Often the real bondage from which we seek release is too private for us to discuss. The urgency of that need drives us onward.

Many women with whom I counsel tell of their enslavement to guilt and fear. They feel guilty about what they cannot change, and fearful about what they cannot control. Other women tell how they are being held like prisoners behind walls of their childhood memories—wishing they could break loose from them, but can't. While they, as individuals, are pushing to set themselves free, the agony of their hurt persists. Like a mother laboring to give birth to her child, she hopes her next breath will relieve her of the prolonged agony she feels. With each trauma she looks for a "birthing" that never seems to come.

Some traditionalists feel the woman's only place is in her home. There are people on the other end of the spectrum too. They have become extremists, joining the ranks of libertarians, giving women the right to be promiscuous, have abortion on demand, or doing about anything they choose—all under the banner of personal freedom.

Somewhere between these two existing extremes, you and I must find a sense of balance. Surely there is a middle road separating the philosophy of the Dark Ages from our present-day attitude of arrogant flippancy that abdicates our moral and spiritual responsibility toward God, ourselves, and society.

Finding that sense of balance could be the most difficult task facing today's woman. For, once the excruciating pain or longing for freedom hits us, the torture of unmet need could drive us into an undisciplined approach toward life itself. Our methods of searching could easily take us into practices that are unchristian in nature, cause us to take on behavioral patterns that are unethical, and build within us attitudes of arrogant pride.

Once we have begun our feverish search, whether it is spiritual, psychological, or physical, let us never forget: God is the creator of balance! He made day and night, the sunshine and rain, the moon and sun. All life is dependent upon the delicate balance of His universe. Astronauts orbit the earth and are able to reach realms of the unknown, because of God's certain predictability in space. We all know that if the earth were to move from its axis that principle of measurement would go "haywire." This same system holds true in our personal lives. Once we get out of focus with His divine order, our lives are in jeopardy.

Bonnie Sylvia, a close friend of mine, found herself a victim of Christian extremism. It took a while for her to understand the full impact of her entrapment:

> When I attended your weekly Bible class and balance was stressed so heavily, there was a question on my mind. *Big deal—why is this so important?* I kept asking myself. When you, Ruthe, would speak to us about making sure we accepted no doctrinal position unless it was in compliance with the total concept of God's Word, I had a smug attitude. Being a new Christian, I often questioned the "why" of your not stressing some "new-fangled" fad that was sweeping our religious community. There were even times I felt you were being a bit cautious.
>
> Not until our family became involved in a situation that hurt me deeply was I able to understand the principle of balance. Before knowing what was happening, my family was caught talking about spiritual freedom on one hand, while being held in the bondage of another extreme. As a result of our blind faith in one individual, we found our lives out of balance with the whole of God's plan.

Bonnie's search for spiritual freedom was one prompted by her needs, and it was an honest search! For me, it was a different kind of searching. The religious trappings of my early training were heavily based in legalism. Having accepted Jesus as my personal Savior at the age of 8, my tender heart was like a piece of potter's clay, easily molded. The problem was that once that mold had set, there was no growth taking place. The stifling, compartmentalized life I had been taught to live was placing me in a kind of solitary confinement.

Finally, the light shone through. Something began to happen, an awakening took place—but could I break loose? Would I find the spiritual/psychological freedom for which I searched?

I began to slowly inch my way in the direction of personal awareness. Looking in retrospect, I observed certain developmental stages through which I passed in my search for psychological/spiritual healing. Those steps were gradual, but distinct in nature:

1. Moment of awakening and enlightenment of my need.
2. Analysis and questioning of those early value systems and an earnest search for a firm biblical balance in my life.
3. Pursuit of fulfillment and the challenge my needs gave me.
4. The time of reward.

My search for spiritual freedom involved my childhood training. Because of my disillusionment with what I had perceived as contradictions, I questioned my present ability to make decisions. Yet, the challenge of freedom was like a light penetrating the hardened wall of legalism by which I was bound.

You may be where I was, only under a different set of circumstances. I hope you may be prodded into a clearer understanding of God's changing process at work in you. While reading the chapters that follow, keep in mind: Your moment of awakening as it applies to your need, the critical questioning as you seek God's guidance, the challenge of your search, and the rewards it will bring you.

Now, take with me your first giant step toward freedom.

SOMETIMES GOD'S ENLIGHTENMENT COMES
AT THE LEAST EXPECTED MOMENT THROUGH
THE MOST UNLIKELY PERSONS.

Chapter 2

Recognizing
Your Growth Process

Sue Anna tells of her moment of awakening and
how it came during her early years of marriage:

Having been born and raised on a farm, and
living three miles from our small town, I found
my early frame of reference limited to those surroundings. When, because of our family's low
income, I was unable to finish high school, my
self-image was reduced to zero-level; because
of my being taken from school, something inside
me died.

Not until one day, as I sat at a luncheon
dressed to the hilt, wearing my fur coat, still
feeling like the little girl on the farm, did I really

see the light. I knew my moment of awakening
had come! There I was, one of the best-dressed
ladies at the social event; yet with feelings of
inferiority and having little self-worth. The child
in me was trapped, but still controlling my life,
making me feel ill-equipped for the society circle
in which my executive husband's position had
placed me.

When the enlightenment of my psychological
need hit, I knew it was time to make changes.
Somehow, I felt that God was giving me a ray
of hope that would lead me to freedom. Now,
it was up to me to move with that light.

My first step was to enroll in a correspondence
course and finish my high school requirements.
After doing so, I ventured into college, taking
only one class at a time. Eventually, out of my
need, I enrolled in speech class, which was the
door opening me to freedom.

As I sat there listening to Sue Anna speak, observing her self-confident posture, and knowing the
personal acceptance she enjoyed, something "clicked"
inside me. *If that light leading her could move her
away from the timid, shy "little girl" she once was,
surely there is hope for me, too*, I thought to myself.
But Sue Anna's next words stunned me!

My friends didn't understand my need.
Some of them would even say: "I liked you
best the way you were!"

Then I knew that I, like Sue Anna, could not always
expect support from my peers.
To make changes in our lives always produces a

"ripple" effect. Often the feedback is negative. For us these transition points become either challenges or stopgaps to growth. The first steps toward freedom are sometimes filled with difficulty because they force us to move from one point of action to another.

We then begin to move from the image of what others expect of us, or what we think they do, to becoming the women God wants us to be. The growth process affects every part of us: our spirits, our emotional well-being, and our psychological acceptance. Family, peers, and other people around us can see the attitudinal change taking place within us. While there may be a few people who are threatened by our growth, others will be challenged by what they see occurring in us.

Just as Sue Anna challenged me to break loose from the legalistic bonds of my past, we do influence others. We effect changes in them by our behavior, while motivating them to move with us. Not only so, we can draw strength from our own learning experiences as we share them with other people. Paul the apostle related his encounter with Christ, his moment of awakening when struck with blindness on the road to Damascus (Acts 9:22). The most effective women I know are those who have dared face up to their needs and then deal with them.

Elizabeth Elliott, in her book *Slow but Certain Light*, writes about God's enlightenment as a series of slow, progressive acts. We all know that life is experienced in small segments, lived but one day at a time. Thus, growth takes its beginning in us one day at a time. The slow but certain light about which Elizabeth wrote is from God as He seeks to guide us in our daily endeavors. His light comes to us in the dark moments of life, and sometimes in the least expected way, through unlikely persons. And because we are not conditioned to recognize that light, we grope along our dimly lighted path of inferiorities, frustrations, and bondage.

There are also moments when someone else's awakening is linked closely to our willingness to be vulnerable. To suppress our needs and deny they exist blocks our creativity in helping others. This was made real to me in an unexpected way while I was recuperating from surgery in a Los Angeles-area hospital.

In a small reception area just down the hall from my room I sat alone, sorting out my feelings, thanking God for His care. The solitude of the moment was interrupted as a man entered the room and proceeded to sit down beside me.

Looking over to see who the person was, I immediately recognized him as the man who had been pointed out to me by the nurses. He had pushed his wife in her wheelchair up and down the hallway past my room for almost a week. Hospital personnel were in a "stir" because of who they were. The man who had joined me was a Hollywood producer and husband of a well-known movie actress.

Looking down at my feet, pointing to my house slippers, he asked, "Lady, did you just walk past my wife's room?"

"Yes, sir, I did!" was my reply.

"Well, I don't know what this means, but when your feet shuffled past, something inside me prompted my coming to find you. Why are you here? Tell me something about yourself."

Quickly I mentioned my diagnosis and talked of my recovery. Without giving details of medical records we chatted together briefly. I was soon to discover that his wife was working through the same physical complications as I was.

"Would you go with me to my wife's room and talk to her?" the man asked.

Me? I thought to myself. *Every nurse in this hospital has tried to get in to see her, and you are asking me to go!* I knew that only her husband, private nurse, and doctor had been allowed in her room. I was to learn later that the chaplain had tried to talk with her earlier in the day and was asked to leave. The question was: Would she want to talk with me?

I cinched the belt of my green satin robe around my waistline and we started the walk toward his wife's room. As we approached the doorway leading to the place where the actress lay on her bed with a curtain pulled around for privacy, I felt like an intruder. On each side of the door were pieces of surgical tape with messages reading: "Keep out—this means you!" As the two of us stepped inside, her husband, as if apologizing, began the introduction.

"Dear, this is Ruthe. I want you to meet her and let her talk with you." Turning to me, he said, "Tell her—tell her the secret of your inner peace."

For a few moments the air was tense and I wondered, *Will I get kicked out as the priest was?* Then I began telling her of my fears and how God had helped me when I confessed them to Him. She listened closely and begged me to stay longer. Before long, she got up, propped herself against her elbow, and tears began flowing down her face.

"Please, I know you're tired, but can I see you again in the morning?" the actress begged of me.

I made my way to her room the next morning to find her fully dressed for the first time since entering the hospital. She was on her way to my room.

Something had happened to her and I knew it. She never waited for me to inquire about her well-being. Instead, she blurted out these words:

"I found the strength I needed to call upon God. During the early-morning hours I found freedom from my fears, these fears that had immobilized me. Physically I have been ill, as you have, but there was another bondage in which I was being held. Thank God, I'm free."

She reached her long arms upward and, pulling my head closely to hers, wept on my shoulder, and I on hers. We prayed together and I left her waving to me as I checked out of the hospital that day. Her words were ringing in my ears as I heard her say, "I can face it: life, death, whatever, because I'm free!"

There she was, a woman with everything: her wealth, popularity, career, and the envy of those who saw her; but she had *something* which was holding her in its vise-like grip. We've all been there, trying to sort through it all with little hope for survival, but this can be your awakening moment. Once you get through the difficult time you will not only feel good about yourself, you can help others, as well.

Kevin, my grandson, was struggling for acceptance in a new school. His parents were caught in unfortunate circumstances which necessitated Kevin's enrollment in three different schools that year. Being a second grader, having to make new friends every few months, had been difficult for him. His frustrations were mounting and the teacher recognized it. She not only had to discipline him but to give him a lot of personal attention.

A year later, after Kevin had found his place among new friends, he was both well-adjusted and a model student. One day while playing on the bars during recess, he looked over and saw his last year's teacher talking with another student. The boy was being disciplined and the teacher was quietly explaining to him the reason for her actions. Kevin, seeing what was taking place, jumped down from the bars on which he was swinging, ran over to where they were sitting and, looking right into the face of the other student, said, "I know just how you feel. I was the new kid last year and I didn't like it either. I was mad just like you are!"

Then Kevin threw his head into the air, pushed out his chest, and exclaimed, "But just look at me now!"

When I think about Sue Anna and how she surmounted her problems of inferiority, and of the actress with her fears, I want to yell out, "Just look at them now!"

I'm sure it wasn't easy for either of them to take their initial steps toward freedom. For both of them it meant two things: a) taking a good look at their problem and b) doing something about it. For Sue Anna it was enrollment in college, while the actress moved with a spiritual dimension of freedom she had never known. So, whatever the personal bondage you may be facing at this moment, keep on walking toward the light until you too can say, "Just look at me now!"

Point of Action

1. What is the one thing I would most like to change about my life?

2. What did I think about most while reading this chapter, and how does it apply to my need?

3. Do I feel God really wants to help me? If so, how? How can I cooperate with Him?

Read Isaiah 58:8,9; 1 John 1:7.

SOMETIME AND SOMEWHERE, SOMEONE WILL
AFFIRM THE WEAKNESSES WE KNOW WE
HAVE. WE CAN ACCEPT THEM AND FIXATE AT
THAT POINT, OR ELSE MOVE ON TOWARD
PERSONAL GROWTH.

Chapter 3

Learning to Like Yourself

Margo is successful at anything she tries. Whether
the project is cooking for a social gathering, working
on a job or in her home, she has the ability to turn
failure into a smashing success story. Margo isn't the
most attractive or beautifully talented friend I have.
She is not what you would say "always lucky." My
friend just has a knack for getting the most out of life.
What some women would use as an excuse for failure
she accepts as a challenge. That lady has learned
to make her own breaks while creating a positive
environment for growth. She sets the stage for
herself and is unafraid to walk out there and respond to life. Most importantly, Margo has learned
to see herself in a good, well-balanced perspective.

Because she can do so, her life is exhilarating and exciting.

How Do You See Yourself?

Our self-image is the very center of our personality. How we accept ourselves affects every part of our life: our work, our choice of friends, and our ability to make changes and experience personal growth. Self-esteem is an important factor in our life's expectations. If our self-concept is poor, we rarely set goals. But by doing this we find ourselves victims of our own negative thinking. Because we believe we can never accomplish our goals or reach our dreams, we spend much of our energy rationalizing our mental nightmares. Once having found all the reasons we can't do something, it becomes easier to absolve ourselves of any responsibility for what we are or who we think we are. Society then takes the brunt of the blame for not having given us greater opportunities. Or we look at the hereditary factors as the culprit holding us back from life's successes, when in reality heredity has little or nothing to do with self-esteem.

Twin brothers from Palm Beach, Florida, have proven that birth plays little part in the final outcome of our lives. John and Greg Rice are multimillionaires. They are also in much demand as motivational speakers, both in the United States and abroad. One of their favorite sayings is: "Success is from the shoulders up." Their one-liner quips add more zest to a show than that of any comedian I have seen or heard. When Greg talks about being a "creative problem-solver," you know he means it. His brother, John, can stimulate your thinking by just turning his head toward the audience, revealing his mouthful of oversize teeth, while laughing his way through a difficult interview.

You see, John and Greg are unusual in other ways too. They are small men, less than four feet tall. Their parents abandoned them at birth, and, because of their obviously dwarfed size, it became difficult for the State of Florida to find foster parents for them. Finally, after having been legally adopted, they were to be without a mother while still in grade school. The mother died when the brothers were eighth-graders. The father passed away while the boys were in their third year of high school. Left alone without parents, not knowing which direction their lives would take them, they began reading self-help books. Together they decided to strike out on the road toward freedom by first breaking loose from the conceptual image of their physical size.

From this background of physical and social deprivation, John and Greg Rice have become two of the nation's greatest real estate entrepreneurs in this decade of the '80's. No one need talk with them about so-called disadvantages in life or their small stature. They simply do not believe their personal worth is related to body size!

When we are able to perceive ourselves in a positive manner, as the Rice Brothers have seemingly been able to do, we find that self-expression comes much easier. Having a low self-image makes us afraid to voice opinions or give expression to our thoughts because we fear rejection. Our "comfort zone" encompasses only those things we feel sure about. We then take no exciting risks and never involve ourselves in programs for personal growth. Our motto becomes: "There is nothing I can do about it now; it's too late to start."

The most common characteristic of poor self-esteem is made apparent through our lack of self-confidence. There are some typical defensive mechanisms we often employ in order to protect our poor image of self:

1. We become obsessed with a kind of personal introspection. By internalizing the external circumstances of life, we feel that anything negative is directed toward us personally, and so our poor self-image is justified.

The confident person works from an inner principle, outwardly always touching base with life. Unlike the person with a good image, when we perceive ourselves poorly we pull life inward, imprisoning ourselves psychologically, emotionally, and spiritually.

2. When our self-image is viewed poorly we tend to vacillate in decision-making. Our pros and cons are weighed with such long and endless questionings that our energies are spent in obsessive trivialities.

3. Seeing ourselves in a negative manner makes it most difficult to assimilate knowledge and to feel that a positive life includes us. Because we have such an inability to overcome the internal roadblocks as to why we are like we are, we hold back our own personal fulfillment. Cicero once said, "All life is mirrored in our minds." Solomon put it even more succinctly when he stated, "As a man thinketh in his heart, so is he" (Proverbs 23:7 KJV).

Where Did You Get Your Self-Image?

Harry Stack Sullivan, a psychologist, thinks of the first months and years of a child's life as being the most critical time in terms of that infant's future self-image. As the child feels the mother's touch, he affirms the "good me" inside himself. Sullivan believes that if the youngster feels loved and lovable, those same feelings are carried into adulthood. While we cannot be sure just how much of our self-concept is predetermined before adolescence, we do know that negative conditioning can affect us for an entire lifetime. The impressions of early childhood do linger with us. A friend of mine tells this story about how she was made to believe she didn't count.

During my fourth year in school my mother became critically ill. My parents were poor people, unable to hire any household help, so my sisters and I had to dress ourselves before going off to school each day. I had gone into the classroom early one morning and seated myself at my desk in the rear of the building. When the bell rang and classes were about to begin, the teacher called me to the front of the room. Pointing down at my dirty, torn tennis shoes, she turned to the other students and said, "Look at this! Is this any way for a student to come to my school?" At that very moment my heart sank right to the bottom of my old tennis shoes. My self-image was tied into as many knots as the strings that held my feet inside those canvas shoes. I knew that no matter how hard I tried, that teacher would never like me, nor I her. I ended up ditching lots of school and eventually dropping out, simply because of my terribly poor self-image.

The tragedy of that story is that the woman believed what her teacher said, even long after she was grown and raising a family. In spite of being the sole beneficiary of her uncle's large estate, she still views herself as the ragged little girl in torn tennis shoes. Her lifestyle, and that of her family, is centered around the "comfort zone" of her knotted conceptions toward life.

Your Self-Image Is Not Cast in Stone

The woman who sat in the seat next to me on the plane was a very attractive person. It was obvious to me by listening to her articulate grammar and observing her actions that she was a woman of some training. When she began talking about her work among the so-called mentally handicapped I was astounded.

> I have learned that instead of a mental deficiency in the people with whom I work, it is a rather poor self-image problem. Children come into my classes unable to read the most elementary books. After working with them for a while, allowing them to feel that they are making progress, stroking them for what they are achieving, I find that they begin to improve. The higher I am able to raise their self-image the faster the pace of their work progresses.

You may be wondering: *How does all of this apply to me?* Who among us has never been discouraged by the hand of another person? We all have! Sometime, or somewhere, someone will cause us to feel we don't count. They will affirm the weaknesses we already know we have. Not one of us is immune to these people. Joyce Landorf labels these people as being "your irregular person." Whoever that individual is, or however that person might make you feel, he or she has the problem—not you! You alone can determine how much of what you hear and see of life will be integrated into your psychological framework. If you are being, or have been, humiliated by a teacher, friend, or member of the family, begin now toward protecting yourself from that negative conditioning.

Five Steps Toward Growth

1. *Take a good look at the people with whom you tend to surround yourself: your friends, associates, and others.* Ask yourself, "Do they make me feel secure in who I am? Do they struggle with the same feelings of insecurity as I?" If so, it is highly possible that you are creating an environment that nurtures your negative feelings. Try making at least one new friend a year. Move out into another circle of people and begin learning the secrets of their survival.

2. *Watch what you say about yourself.* Keep a mental record of how often you say yes to any ideas that would challenge you.

3. *Identify your good characteristics.* Now don't say you have none! Go ahead and write them down, listing those things about yourself that you would like if found in one of your friends. Look at what skills you might have, and work hard in developing a specific area of your life.

4. *Be determined to rise above your present level.* Involve yourself with someone else's problems and help solve them.

5. *Let go of yourself by releasing your feelings, whatever they may be, into God's hands.* Give the situation to Him through an effort of commitment.

Imagine that you are holding the deepest hurt of

your life in the palms of your hands. Call it by name, or verbally recite the experience you are encountering. Tell Jesus exactly how you feel about it. Or, if you feel resentment against someone who is making you (or has made you) feel less than good, relate those pent-up hurts to Him. Tell the Lord you are tired of carrying the weight of your hangups, and ask Him to take them away from you. Once that is done, turn your outstretched hands upside down and pray this simple prayer:

> God, I give this to You. Help me to never be guilty of accepting this burden back into my life. When I am tempted, for I know I shall be, remind me of this prayer and give me the grace needed to overcome my problem.

As you look at your outstretched hands turned downward, you will realize that you can hold nothing in them. It is the giving, the total surrender, to God that brings healing. Healing them becomes the first step toward building a new and positive self-image. After having done this, you will need to put yourself in a healing environment. Just as a plant requires water, air, and light for growth, there are ingredients necessary for our personal development. You need a combination of factors intellectually, psychologically, and spiritually that will stimulate your growth process.

Intellectually we find growth in being with people. Whatever interests or hobbies you may have in life, don't be afraid to pursue them. I know a minister who was nearing retirement age with almost nothing to assure him of his future security. He had been a collector of old classic golf clubs for years, since a very young man, and the knowledge acquired throughout his life was invaluable. When he realized there were no retirement funds for him, he set out to do something about it. Moving from a highly visible position as a successful pastor to a nonentity was not good for his self-concept. He found himself without the respect shown a clergyman, living in a new community where few people knew or cared about his exceptional pastoral record. Rather than sit down and do nothing, he decided to put his knowledge to work. He opened a small business, first selling golf clubs from his years of collecting, later moving into customizing a line of golf products. Within five years his business had grown to the point of enabling him to sell out as a financially secure individual.

Learning to Like Yourself

Learning to like yourself enables you to love other people more freely. By loving you will be loved! This can be made possible only by having an insight into God's loving nature toward you. In my book *Touch Me Again, Lord* (Here's Life Publishers), I talk about how we know He loves us. There are three ways in which we may identify God's work within our lives: by knowing that a) He believes in us, b) He identifies with us, and c) He invests His nature within us, making it possible to succeed in our endeavors.

Joni, the teenager calling me on the telephone, could not believe the aforementioned principles. She was pleading for help.

"How do I break away from my self-hate? Why do you keep telling me God loves me, when no one else does? I certainly do not love myself! No one could love a drug addict like me, not even God."

"Well," I said to her, "I can tell you that God loves you until you turn blue in the face, but my words will not help you one bit until you make some personal decisions. You must believe this for yourself."

Joni's personal appearance, her lifestyle, and everything about her perpetuated her low self-image. However, that's not the end of her story. I met Joni at a church convention recently. For a moment I didn't recognize the young woman I was seeing. Her hair was neatly combed and she was immaculately dressed.

When I finally came to believe that I was lovable, that God could and did love me, other people began treating me in a loving manner. Drugs are now in my past— an image I would like to leave behind. I am getting my life turned around, and now I see myself as a worthwhile person.

You, like Joni, must decide with an act of your own will to believe that God will make changes for you.

FORMULA: Your WILL wills to believe that God WILL!

Once you choose to move away from the past of your conditioning, you're headed for freedom!

Point of Action

1. Why is self-acceptance so important in our relationship with Christ?

2. What is meant by Jeremiah 38:11?

3. How do we apply "God's righteousness," according to 1 John 2:29?

   A. Whose righteousness is it?

   B. When do we merit His gifts?

   C. Who must accept the gift of righteousness?

4. Who is responsible in changing our self-image? What part do you have in making a change?

5. Who does God say you are?

John 11:52

Galatians 3:26

1 Thessalonians 5:5

3 John 4

STEP II

DARE TO CHANGE

...don't be afraid...for I, the Lord, will
be with you and see you through.

Jeremiah 1:8

WE MAY NOT ALWAYS KNOW WHERE THE
DIVIDING LINE IS BETWEEN OUR NEEDS AND
OUR PLEASURABLE WANTS, BUT WE USU-
ALLY KNOW WHEN WE HAVE CROSSED OVER
THE BOUNDARIES.

Chapter 4

Taking Control
of Your Life

Somewhere between fulfillment and an attitude of
selfish egotism there is a very thin line. Balancing our
needs across that invisible mark may be as difficult
as walking the proverbial tightrope. While we may
not always be able to distinguish where the dividing
line is between our pleasurable wants and our needs,
we do usually know when we have crossed the
boundaries. We know because our psychological self
gets out of balance with the rest of life. When fulfillment is pursued to the exclusion of all other felt needs,
we are in trouble! Learning how to live following our
dreams, but doing so without neglect of meaningful
priorities, is one of the most difficult challenges that
today's woman will encounter.

One of the greatest fallacies of the feminist move-ment of the past few decades has been in encourag-ing women to go out and "find themselves" at any cost. They did not give us all the facts. We were not told that if we sought careers, married, and had children, we would be no more immune to family stress than any other woman. They didn't forewarn us that our children were not exempt from catching measles, chicken pox, or any other childhood disease floating through the air. Neither did the feminists mention that our children might spend a restless, feverish night, needing our care, to be followed by a day of work on our jobs. Because of this kind of blind conditioning urging us to leave our homes, find meaningful careers, and forget about marriage and childbearing, we have begun to approach life through an unrealistic expectation level.

Our Inability

Psychologically we are not able to meet the demands that society is placing upon us. These unreal expectations are being imposed upon us from all segments of society. Psychologically we are ready to make a change, but we may not fully understand where that change is taking us. There is such a demanding attitude on the part of society that makes us feel we are to be the Superwoman of our day. The "Superwoman Syndrome" is one with which we have all had to learn to cope. While we may not fully understand the pressures of why we have to be the best in everything, we know the pressure is there.

It has been this strong-woman concept that has made us think through other issues pertaining to our homes and families. While many in the early formation of the liberation movement minimized the role of the woman in the home (feeling it to be one of the greatest deterrents to a woman's fulfillment), they are now doing some backtracking on the matter. Betty Friedan, author and early leader of the group, deals with the error of their judgments in her book *The Second Stage*. In this book the author points out the fallacies of those assumptions as related to the woman's role in the home. She also talks about women who wish to reprioritize family relationships in their own lives.

Betty, who along with others once seemed to feel that all a woman needed to do for fulfillment was to go out and find herself a job drawing equal pay with her male counterparts, is now admitting that something went awry in their philosophical thinking. The Utopia of their once-promised freedom held inconsistencies as related to the real issues of life. Friedan recognizes that those women who had once felt trapped in their homes are now being met with a new set of problems: They are having to juggle careers along with other responsibilities with which they had failed to reckon. These women who were determined to "find themselves" at any cost are now facing decisions of childbearing and are struggling to find "prime time" for raising children they plan on having.

According to Sheila Kamerman, Professor of Social Policy at Columbia University of Social Work, today's woman, even though she is working, is becoming more family-oriented, seeking to find quality time for her offspring. Also, in spite of the fact that women are having less leisure time of their own, they still seek to give "family time" a top priority. Why has this principle resurfaced?

We all know that the basic needs of our lives are

first met within the context of the family structure. Though in some cases the home and family does not supply all the loving support that is needed, it is nevertheless the foundational base upon which civilization survives. Not only so, but the home provides us with a great sense of belonging. You remember that it was God who first made a home for mankind. When He put Adam and Eve in the Garden, it was a place that He had prepared for them. That Garden was intended for their pleasure, for fellowship, and for living!

In our homes we form the oldest and most lasting friendships. If we are fortunate enough to have brothers or sisters, they become the first real friends we have. Not only so, but the longer each one lives, the stronger that bond of friendship lasts—provided it is nourished. Our family ties are often the strongest bonds that will develop during a lifetime. To minimize the need for this caring relationship within the family unit is to put oneself off-center from the basic psychological needs of life. Once there is an estrangement from within the family structure, everyone involved becomes the loser.

Burt Reynolds, actor and producer, spoke recently about his struggle with a recent illness. Burt had been sick over a period of time and was talking about how he needed the folks back home. When asked if there had been any changes in his life during his brief illness, Burt replied:

> Yes, I call home more often. I have learned to appreciate those people who are close to me even more, especially my dad and mom.

To pursue fulfillment at the cost of these relationships makes us vulnerable to our emotions, leaving us in a psychological vacuum, a "hungry mode" in the computer of time.

A woman stood in line against the wall of the retreat building where I had just finished speaking. She and several others were waiting their turn to talk with me. By the time she reached me her eyes were moistened with tears as she poured out her heart:

> I am estranged from my daughter. You see, our girl was born with a physical and mental deficiency. Because of her problems it has been difficult for me to discipline her. From the time of her early adolescence she has been an incorrigible child. It seems that her father and I just cannot handle her. Because of this it has been a real effort for me to love her as I should. In fact, Ruthe, it has been over eight years since I have put my arms around my own daughter and told her I loved her. Now I've reached the point of no return, and when I get home I'm taking this overgrown teenager into my arms and tell her how much she is loved.

What had happened in this relationship? Whatever it was, that mother was out of sync with her emotional self, and she knew it would never be righted until she dealt with the problem.

We don't have to be involved in careers to permit our selfish interests to take precedence over the most important aspects of life. But if we allow other things to become top priorities, pushing our marriages and families into second place, we are in big trouble. Just recently I shuddered while listening to a well-known television scriptwriter give his personal philosophy of life:

> Personal fulfillment is my number one need. My work and career come in a close second, with my marriage and wife being considered as third. I consider my marriage as being nothing more than the third party in a working relationship. Any time being married interferes with the aforementioned priority systems of my life, it is over.

The man spoke those words with great emphasis as he talked about his life's philosophy. Human relationships were minimized to second place, if he could only achieve success and self-fulfillment. Still, that man's thinking is not unlike some ideas held within the Christian community. A woman came for counseling and said:

> My husband is not a believer. He doesn't want me to have anything to do with the church and is adamant against my donating so much time working in church-oriented projects. But I don't care what he says—I feel fulfilled in what I am doing. That is where I get my greatest sense of personal satisfaction.

Look at this situation for just a moment. The woman's motive in giving of herself so freely seems to be a commendable trait—that is, on the surface! In order to put her ideas into proper perspective, we must ask some questions: Was the woman giving her time out of love for Jesus Christ, or was her church work providing the excuse needed to get away from an unhappy marriage relationship? The answer to those questions came from the woman herself a few months later. She came back into the office and said:

> Pastor, my husband has left me (praise God!). So now I am free to work for the Lord and find myself a good Christian man whom I can marry.

What a spiritually deceptive idea for personal fulfillment! That woman, like many others I have met, was finding it difficult to differentiate between her psychological needs and her egotistical wants. She had allowed herself to become the victim of her own deception. So long as there have been people we have had that problem! The prophet Jeremiah encountered the same kind of philosophical reasoning when he observed the people of his day. While his words are not too popular in this decade of self-seeking, they are nonetheless relevant. The weeping prophet, having seen all his aching soul could tolerate, cried out in desperation:

> The heart is the most deceitful thing there is, and desperately wicked. No one can really know how bad it is! Only the Lord knows! He searches all hearts and examines deepest motives (Jeremiah 17:9,10).

To examine our motives and deal honestly with ourselves is a near-impossible task. We tend to view life through the backdrop of our psychological, physical, and emotional needs. And because we do, our theology becomes fitted to our needs. It becomes difficult for us to make decisions unless we can weigh our motives on the scale of what is best for the kingdom of God. Even then judgments are often clouded because of our emotions. It is highly possible that the emotional "cup of our lives" may be full and running over, but at the same time we may be empty and void of the Holy Spirit's presence. During these moments life seems to be out of control, simply because God has not been given first place.

The psalmist spoke of this spiritual condition when he recognized the dearth in which the nation of Israel found themselves. A nation whom God brought out of bondage, they were indulging in open rebellion toward both Moses and God. The writer of the psalm, observing their search for the "good life" at any cost, knew that their attitudes had placed them out of balance with what God desired for them:

> He gave them their demands, but sent them leanness in their souls (Psalm 105:15).

There will be times when God will permit us to go out there and get what we want—anything our hearts desire—but we do so at great spiritual risk. Since we cannot leave the decision-making of our lives up to our emotional whims, what is the basis upon which we must determine our life?

1. Face up to any clear-cut directives that are in the Word of God concerning the situation of your life.

2. If there are no defined guidelines, remember that God works within a balanced perspective of His kingdom.

3. No amount of rationalization will change what God has determined. Therefore it becomes necessary for us to base our lifestyles and decision-making upon biblical principles.

At this point, you may be faced with a decision that looks profitable from a point of human reasoning. Still, in your heart you know that the ultimate end of your choice will not further God's cause. To consider the fleeting benefits of a psychological choice outside the guidelines of a balanced biblical principle is sure to bring you a delayed heartbreak. You may even now be grappling with a broken relationship that is tearing you apart. If so, you can do something about it. Begin now to make an effort to restore the relationship. Perhaps it's a parent, a brother, a sister, or a child; whomever it may be, you can get your life back on dead center. It can be done by rebuilding those rightful priorities. God will enable you to do it if you will put forth the energy.

1. Begin today toward making the effort.

2. Don't be discouraged if you seem rejected.
3. Let time heal your wounds.

A mother in Northern California attended a seminar where I was teaching. At the close of the meetings she gave this testimony:

> I was raised in Spain. My father was a wealthy cattle rancher. He was very demanding, and controlled us children by his hot-tempered words. I was afraid of him and left home because of it. As a girl of 16 I walked out of our home, found myself a job, and soon married. The man I wed was a serviceman, and he brought me to the United States. We later had three children, and then he divorced me, leaving me alone in a new country. The years that followed were difficult. In the meantime, when I heard from any member of my family, they always told me that Papa would never recognize me as being his daughter. Contacts with my family were minimal, since they were still living in Spain.
>
> Then one day I took my children to church. It was at this time that I accepted Christ as my personal Savior. The more I grew in the Lord, the more I wanted to restore the broken relationship I had with my father. Somehow I felt I had to get to him, to ask his forgiveness for hurting him and leaving the family as I did. But there seemed to be no possible way! The more I prayed about it, the more I was convinced that it was something I had to do: Go and witness to my father about God's saving grace in my life. The church I attend caught my burden and took

an offering, permitting my return to the country of my birth.

When I arrived I was not sure just what would happen. After spending several days with a brother, I knew that it was time to make that effort. As I approached the door of the old homeplace, my father was seated inside. He had already been informed of my coming but refused to open to me, saying, "I have no daughter by your name." Finally, after much persuasion, he agreed to let me enter the house, all of the time cursing me for what I had done to him. My heart was aching for the father who felt so mistreated, and for the man who knew nothing about my newfound salvation. After standing there for a long time, I walked over to him and threw my arms around him, crying out, "Daddy, I love you. I am sorry, so sorry, for the hurt I have caused you." He pushed me away from him as if in utter disgust. Eventually I was able to speak with Dad, but only on limited terms.

When I left Spain I went away with a broken heart, knowing that my father was getting to be an old man and would soon die. *Would I ever see him again? Did he hate me, as I felt he did?* These were the questions that flooded my mind. My only hope was in knowing how much I had tried.

Dad died a short time later, and my family called, asking me to return home for his burial. After we had taken care of the final arrangements of business, and I was preparing to return home, a brother insisted that I stay longer. Not knowing why he was so persistent, and needing to get back to the children in the States, I proceeded with my previous plans to fly home. My brother finally turned to me and said, "Sister, I know you are unaware that Dad included you in his will. You are now a wealthy woman. From the day you came and threw your arms around him he became a different man. You, whose name could not be mentioned in our household, have become the beneficiary of much of his estate."

Yes, time and God take care of a lot of things! Problems often keep us from making the decisions that would restore us to our families and friends . . . and to our heavenly Father. But once we make the effort, what a liberating experience it becomes!

Point of Action

Do you feel estranged from a relative, a friend, or someone you love?

Fill out this form:

PERSON _____

Why do I feel this way?

What is my real feeling?

How do I think he/she feels?

What prompts his/her reactions?

How can I better understand him/her?

How do I really feel?

Read Proverbs 10:12; 27:10; Ecclesiastes 4:9,10;
Luke 19:8; Mark 11:25; Ephesians 4:32.

GOD'S ACCEPTANCE OF US IS NOT BASED ON OUR MUSCLE TONE OR CONTOURS. HE JUST LOVES AND ACCEPTS US FOR WHAT WE ARE AND CAN BECOME!

Chapter 5

Accepting Your Better Self

Let's face it—not many of us are the modellike women so often depicted on television. Most of us fight the "Battle of Cellulite." Even when we exercise, we don't look like the pencil-thin aerobics teacher who instructs us on "how to lose it all."

There has been such a thrust toward weight loss over the past few years that to be a few pounds overweight marks us as an undisciplined, overindulgent Christian. While it is true that the Bible teaches "temperance in all things," there are no Scriptures that lay out a formula of 36, 26, 36 as being the ticket getting us acceptance into heaven.

You may be one of those persons who can keep a wellbalanced figure, eat right, exercise daily, and maintain the svelte physical appearance you've always had. But please be patient with those of us who can't. Some of us cannot shed poundage as quickly as others. Even after having done all everyone else does, that seems to make little difference in our weight loss.

In this decade, with so much emphasis being placed on thinness, a kind of epidemic is sweeping through the country. One movie actress purportedly stated, "All fat people should be locked up." Unwittingly, there seems to be much the same attitude among those within the Christian community.

This is not meant to minimize the wonderful advantages of any exercise program offering assistance. I love being a part of the aerobics culture. What I don't like is when we bring it into our churches, labeling it "spirituality." By so doing we become extremists, placing into bondage the woman who can't get her body weight down. She feels guilty and highly uncomfortable in the presence of her trim sisters. Let us not forget:

1. Spirituality is not measured by muscle tone.
2. God's acceptance of us is not determined by our poundage or contours.
3. We are valued for what we are.

While I am sure that no one would attempt to discredit our relationship with God on the basis of appearance, there is an underlying attitude that troubles me. So much emphasis upon human perfection can be misleading and hurtful. Who sets the standards? Are they the same for everyone? These are some of the questions that should be asked, both of ourselves and others. Within the church community particularly is a responsibility toward both self-improvement and tolerance. We need to do all we can with what God gives us. And there is no excuse for letting the package He wrapped us in become torn and frayed. We don't need to have that "run-over-at-the-heels" look to be spiritual. At the same time, too much emphasis is being placed on appearance.

The fact that some women suffer from an inability, because of medical reasons, to attain that preset image of loveliness should make us more tolerant toward their needs. You may be one of those persons. Fortunately for me, I have always been able to maintain reasonably good weight control without a great deal of effort. But I have friends who, if they ate as many calories a day as I do, would be obese. If you happen to be one of those persons struggling with a weight problem and a low self-image problem, take heart! Susan Wooley, in a survey for *Glamour* magazine, talks about our contemporary obsession with weight as a perversion of feminism (*MS*, May 1985). She speaks of thinness as being "a cultural symbol of competency."

In a recent poll, among those women who were asked, "What is your greatest fear?" 38 percent answered, "The fear of getting fat." However, there is another side to this coin. Ernsberger of the National Institute of Health shows that a little weight can be helpful in disease resistance. He also found in a heart study that the rate of cancer decreased in women who were just above the "correct" weight given in most insurance manuals. Women in the Ernsberger studies also indicated a lower mortality rate among those with a little more weight than those whose poundage was within the "desirable weight" category. It is so easy for us to become victims of some "thing," often to the point of guilt!

The Youth Syndrome

We not only don't want to gain weight, but we are obsessed with the "youth syndrome." No mentally healthy individual is looking forward to old age. On the other hand, no healthy person can deny its inevitability. When we consider the alternative to aging, most of us prefer longevity instead. The emphasis on youth faces us at each turn of our lives. It has become a pressure point at work and for acceptance in life. Not long ago a minister friend sent his resume to a church board, who later informed him that no one past age 50 was being interviewed. Since we live in such a youth-oriented society, we seem to have no other option than to do everything within our power to maintain a youthful appearance. It becomes a means of survival, at least in some cases.

Women reaching their middle years become victims of themselves, obsessed with how they look. With such unreasonable demands upon today's woman, it drives some beyond their physical, financial, or psychological limits. When we try to live within that "Ideal Image," we are denying a basic psychological fact of life: the aging process!

Pressures on the Emotional Self

Everywhere the push is to be more, get more, accomplish more, and deserve more. "Life owes you more than this" has become the theme song of the '80's. This constant bombardment is placing pressures upon us that were once unheard of. There is a rapidly growing concept of materialism sweeping across the religious community as well.

Christians are not much different from the rest of society. A recent study by a marketing expert revealed that we as Christians are now approaching life with the same self-indulgent attitude as the rest of the world. In fact, this researcher called us "Hellenistic," with little relationship between what we believed theologically and the manner in which we actually lived.

Often it is difficult for us to distinguish between what we want and what our needs really are, so we work harder, driving ourselves to get more things. The dividing line of balance is becoming more difficult to determine. Since we live in an immoral society, ethical codes are being drawn out like a fishing line on a reel. Methods for "pulling in the fish" are sometimes as questionable as the catch we are hauling in. This materialistic kind of attitude is made evident in many ways. We were made aware of this recently while trying to sell our home. The house was listed with a local real estate broker. He had shown the property and called us, feeling sure of a quick sale.

> My client is a lovely Christian woman,
> and she wants your house. She says she
> has prayed about it and that God has told
> her she should have it at this price.

Her offer was embarrassingly low as compared to the market selling price. Still, the man insisted that his client should have the house because "she is a deeply religious woman."

When he had finished talking, Claude told him:

You know something? My wife and I are God's children too. And we don't think God is in the business of ripping off one of His kids to give it to another.

Needless to say, the house sold at a later date, but not to that lady! Some Christian friends bought it at a fair price for both them and us. We can't afford, as Christian women, to let the fishing reel of our religious pride place its hook into a selfish principle that is going to destroy another person's individual rights. No amount of social pressure invalidates the principle of God's Word. The only balancing instrument is found in the Golden Rule: "Do as we would have others do unto us."

Even when coming from a church background, we find it easy to measure our decisions upon some faddish approach within our religious "comfort zone." Sometimes there may even be a degree of comfort connected with what we are doing, or seek to be engaged in, because it is condoned by society. This approach may seem all right on the surface but actually be completely outside the demand of Christ for our lives.

THE COMFORT ZONE

1. Everyone else is doing it.
2. I'm better than the average person.
3. Why not?

To move out of that cozy circle of self-pleasing is to challenge ourselves into becoming more than we presently are. Once we do so, we will discover a sense of personal freedom.

Point of Action

1. In what way is inferiority a form of pride?

2. What is the difference between true humility and self-acceptance?

3. How does "truth" set us free, as in John 8:32?

4. Why does inferiority produce hostility?

   Romans 9:1-3

   Psalm 34:2

   Isaiah 45:9

5. What happens when we try to compare ourselves with other people?

BLIND FAITH IN HUMAN LEADERSHIP ALWAYS
LEADS US INTO SPIRITUAL OPPRESSION.

Chapter 6

Developing the Spiritual Self

Nestled in the foothills of Southern California is a lovely church with a cross towering above its gabled front. On smoggy days the sanctuary is visible but the cross on top is obscured by the haze of California smog. Like the smoky layer of gray fumes that hides the face of the cross atop the little church, there is a condition existing in this twentieth century that makes it difficult to view Christ through the eyes of our spiritual freedom.

We are often blinded by the spiritual elitism filtering through the air! We see it exemplified in the Christian celebrity status so prevalent among us. There are a few religious leaders who have set themselves up as authorities in the written Word. Among this group so much emphasis is being placed upon "my ministry" that we are beginning to wonder, *Where does the cross come into focus?* Obscured within the layers of "I-ism," the message of Christ is sometimes lost.

Out of this environment two problems are developing: a) There is a tendency among some people who having been made free in Christ Jesus, to put themselves under a different kind of bondage; b) by relinquishing their personal liberty to the credo of a religious leader or faddish philosophy, they make themselves victims. Sometimes they tend to become more fiercely loyal to a leader than to the cause of Christ. This condition is similar to that of the early New Testament church. When the apostle Paul went to visit his converts in Corinth he found them choosing up sides with their favorite speakers. Some believers were standing with him, while others affirmed their allegiance to another man whose name was Apollos. Paul dealt with the issue by helping the newborn Christians refocus their attention toward the cross:

> It is from God alone that you have life through Christ Jesus. He showed us God's plan of salvation; he was the one who made us acceptable to God; he made us pure and holy and gave himself to purchase our salvation (1 Corinthians 1:30).

Today's women, and others, are confused between "who's who" in churchdom, and tend to become dependent upon the person in leadership. They often accept carte blanche whatever is being taught. "After all," they ask themselves, "who am I to question such a great (wo)man of God?" They swallow whatever is being said without cutting through the fog to see if the cross is centered within the message. Paul forewarned us about the possibility of being duped by those parading in angels' costumes. Knowing our human tendency to be deceived, he said:

> You seem so gullible: you believe what-
> ever anyone tells you even if he is preach-
> ing about another Jesus than the one we
> preach, or a different spirit than the Holy
> Spirit you received, or shows you a differ-
> ent way to be saved. You swallow it all (2
> Corinthians 11:4).

Freedom's Trappings

Our Christian freedom is often draped in robes of self-righteousness. We cover ourselves in self-righ-teousness, believing that freedom is found in works alone. Like the Pharisees in Jesus' day, who sewed wide pieces onto their garments to show how pious they were, we demonstrate the same kind of selfish religiosity. But instead of standing on the street corners reciting long prayers, we talk about how spiritual we are. In my brief history of church involvement, never have I heard more "chatter-eze" than is being heard now. The religious horizon is filled with it! Everyone seems to have "a word" for someone else, with the weaker personality being dominated by the stronger. The spiritual elitists are always giving direction to someone else, and their advice is too often followed without questioning.

A couple in this area were once told by one of their leaders to move from their present place of employ-ment to another. Without seeking direction or confirmation from God for themselves, they packed the family belongings and headed out. Two years later they returned to our city disillusioned with life, not understanding what had happened and wanting nothing to do with Christianity.

Here was a lovely family who had become victims of an oppression cloaked in religious overtones. There was just enough "Christianeze" to make them feel comfortable in what they thought was the right thing to do. Many people among us simply cannot face up to the fact that there are manipulators within the church circle whose purpose is to put us under bondage to them. They are bent on taking away our freedom, binding us under the old laws of legalism. Listen to the words of the apostle Paul:

> Christ has made us free. Now make sure that you stay free and don't get all tied up again in the chains of slavery (Galatians 5:1).

A Form of Cultism

Christ in His earthly ministry drew an analogy from what He was seeing. One day while walking through the streets of the city He observed two things happening. On one side was a group of children playing in the street, blowing noises through their long bamboo reeds in a make-believe celebration. Across from them stood a group of religious people of His time. They were haggling over some technicality of the law. Jesus, turning to them, said:

> What shall I say about this nation? These people are like children playing, who say to

their little friends, "We played wedding and
you weren't happy, so we played funeral
but you weren't sad" (Matthew 11:16,17).

Like children in the marketplace, we may find
ourselves being asked to celebrate, to play games on
the streets of the religious community. Not only so,
but there are a lot of mind tactics that are being used
as incentives.

Ten Games People Play

1. Ask me and I will tell you what God wants you
to know.
2. How can you question what I am saying? Do you
doubt that I am called of God?
3. Give to my ministry because I am the only one
teaching truth.
4. Do as I tell you and God will bless you!
5. You don't need to seek God's will for your life
because you are His will. Whatever you wish to do
is okay with Him.
6. Intercessory prayer is not necessary today.
7. Since you are no longer living under the Old
Testament Law, the Ten Commandments are not
relevant to twentieth-century living.
8. Follow me and I will make you spiritual, prosper-
ous, and to be envied.
9. When you accept Jesus Christ your problems are
over. You will become healthy, wealthy, and wise.
You will never struggle or hurt!
10. If you are in the will of God, no adversity, sickness, or problems will come to you. If you *are* sick,
you are not in the faith, or there is sin in your life.

On the surface of each argumental game can be found some degree of biblical principle. But where we find our greatest danger is in giving other persons a blank sheet of paper and allowing them to inscribe their signature across our rights for spiritual freedom. When our liberty is dictated through the private interpretations of another person's theology, we are in bondage! Once this occurs, we become victimized by a cultic dogma emerging from a hotbed of blind acceptance. That is exactly what happened in the Jim Jones incident in Guyana.

Need we be reminded that in the Jones case his group of loyal followers minimized their God-given ability for reasoning, and instead turned over their intellectual powers to a man obsessed by his own inerrancy? The problems come when a person (or group of persons) takes a principle from the Word and puts a private interpretation upon it, declaring it to be God's law.

Once a law is established, someone must be responsible, and it is usually a self-appointed person who becomes the arbitrator of this law. He then sets himself up as judge and juror, keeping other people on trial. One person begins to feel himself capable of invoking the sentence upon another when a law is broken. How easy it is to get under bondage to the ideas of another person!

We as women dare not permit a few self-proclaimed prophets to put us under their kind of servitude. We saw this happen during the '70's, when a great thrust for women's submission hit the church. (Of course we believe the scriptural approach to submission, but it went beyond that.) There were leaders in the Christian community who carried that principle to a point of total psychological devastation, placing women under a form of spiritual bondage. One group in a northern state took the biblical concept so far as to have formal rituals in which the woman would lie down on the floor, allowing her husband to put his foot across her neck as a symbol of total submission to him. During that time I counseled with many younger women who, in their great desire to follow God, did all the things these leaders asked of them. As a result they soon lost all self-identity and became nothing more than a pawn of someone else's philosophy.

Blind faith in human leadership always leads to spiritual oppression. On the other hand, if we can cut our way through all the theological haze and find the point of the cross, we will experience freedom, a liberation from our past, healing for hurts, and guidance for the future.

Point of Action

Here are three ways to test a principle or faddish philosophy. Ask yourself:

1. Have I taken the Bible and studied the principle for myself, earnestly seeking God's direction? If so, can I honestly say that the idea is based on total compliance with Scripture?

2. Could this be applied and made workable if taught anywhere in the world? Is it universal in scope or is it limited to our cultural setting? If it does not

meet the needs of all persons, regardless of where they might live, you can rest assured that it is in conflict with God's purpose upon earth.

3. Is the principle a balanced concept found in both the Old and New Testaments, or have a few isolated Scriptures been taken out of context and used to prove a point?

Read Psalm 73:24; Proverbs 2:6; 3:13; James 1:5; John 16:13; Luke 11:4; 2 Timothy 3:6.

STEP III

COUNT THE COST

O Lord, I know it is not within the power of man to map his life and plan his course— so you correct me, Lord; but please be gentle.

Jeremiah 10:23,24

GOD DID NOT CREATE US TO BECOME SUB-
JECTS OF TYRANNY BUT TO BE FREE CREA-
TURES: FREE TO BE CREATIVE, TO GROW AND
REACH OUR FULL POTENTIAL IN HIM.

Chapter 7

Your Personal Need

You can tell when a woman feels she has personal
freedom! There is something about the way she walks,
the spring in her step, and the sparkle in her eye that
reveals it. When she feels less than free, that too
shows in her every movement: Her shoulders droop,
there is a slow unsteadiness about the way she moves,
and her emotional stride is off-rhythm with life's
surroundings.

The same is true with each of us, both male and
female; we don't face life easily when we know there
are threats against our freedom. There is a reason
we don't function well under these circumstances: It
is because God did not create us to become subjects
of tyranny. He made us to be free creatures—free

to be creative, to grow and reach our fullest potential in HIM!

We are born with a free spirit. It is not until we have learned fear that we feel less than free. The newborn child knows no barriers to his or her freedom. The child's natural inclination is to follow his curious yearnings in the exploration of life.

If there is a question on this matter of freedom, it is not "Do we all seek freedom?" Instead, the question is *"How?"* How do we find that individual freedom so necessary for productive living? While seeking to find those answers, we are free to pursue many avenues within the searching process. Some paths may lead us to a growth relationship with God and an ongoing understanding of ourselves, while others take us to a dead-end street. Many roads are marked "Freedom This Way." Still, we know they do not always lead us to the fulfillment we seek.

Based upon this great need to live without human restraints, today's woman has surmounted many obstacles in order to make her life's position secure.

The Universal Need

This need for personal fulfillment is one that is universal in scope. Not only does the need for freedom encompass the globe, but there is no way to predict people's response when those freedoms are being threatened. We need only to look at a page from our own history to understand this principle more clearly. Our forebears braved the ocean's danger for the sake of religious freedom. They did so with courage, at the risk of their own lives. The risks were immeasurable, but were undertaken with bravery! The struggle for freedom, whether as a universal or an individual effort, is uniquely real. We all know that the drive to be free and live without enslavement is a motivating force in the human response mechanism. We are also aware that there are no scientific instruments that can accurately measure the strength of the human will for survival. This was a factor that historians tell us the Japanese overlooked when they declared war on the United States.

When the Japanese dropped the first bombs on Pearl Harbor, on December 7, 1941, they failed to take into account the will of the American people. The Japanese regime ordered the attack against us with full knowledge of their ultimate aim—to bring our nation under the dictatorial reign of Japan. What the Japanese could never understand was our people's need for freedom. They never took into consideration our dogged determination as Americans to keep ourselves a free nation under God. Prior to that time, no other nation during U.S. history who had first been attacked by another country had won a war.

Whether the need for freedom is a collective one (as with our nation in World War II) or an individual one, when the will to fight is broken, those persons become victims of prey. Once the spirit of an individual has been beaten down, there is little hope for survival. No doubt this is what the writer of Proverbs meant when he stated, "A man's courage can sustain his broken body, but when courage dies, what hope is left?" (Proverbs 18:14).

Just as no one can know the depths of despair into which a discouraged woman may find herself when hope has vanished, neither can anyone calculate the actions of a courageous woman. I am sure no one could have imagined that Florence Nightingale would jump astride a horse and run through the battle, helping to secure the freedom of her people. There are simply no known barriers that we will not attempt to break through for the cause of personal freedom!

You may have heard the movie, about the family living in Czechoslovakia at the time the Communists overran that country. A young man by the name of Robert Hutyra felt that his freedom would soon be taken from him, so he devised a plan for escape. Having read something about an air balloon, he reasoned that by building one it would be an escape to safety. He tried once but failed in his attempt to get it skyward. The fabric from which the balloon was made had needle holes at each seam, allowing the wind to pass through the canopy. But Hutyra and his wife, Jana, would not be defeated. Even though their resources were depleted, they continued in their laborious efforts to find a way out of the country. Finally, after having borrowed enough money to purchase another fabric (a durable cloth from which raincoats were made), the couple finished the project. The home in which they lived was put up for sale under the false pretense of their being transferred to another city for work. When the property sold, they were able to load their belongings into the car without causing undue suspicion from the townspeople.

Still not knowing if the plan would work, the Hutyras drove away to a preplanned place of departure, where they were hoping for enough wind to carry them to safety. The makeshift apparatus was limited in the amount of cargo it would carry. The basket in which the family—Robert, Jana and their two children, were to ride was no larger than one square yard of platform space.

Under shelter of the evening light, Robert attached

the car's exhaust inside the balloon, filling it with air. Tied onto the edges of the grilled basket were the four gas tanks that would heat the air. When the heavy fabric began to shoot upward, Robert lighted the first burner and Jana severed the ropes that held it to the ground. After much difficulty, and a near loss to their lives, they began the ascent. Rising higher and higher with the aid of the wind currents, they soon reached a height of almost 8000 feet. Being airborne for some time and not knowing where they were going to land, the Hutyra family could only hope for enough gas in the small tanks to carry them across the Czecho-slovakian border. Finally they saw the lights of a city below them. Hoping that they were landing in a country that would give them freedom, but not knowing for sure, they decided to land.

The Hutyras turned off the burners and began their descent. They could only hope that they would be setting foot in a new country, one that would give them political freedom.

Soon they could see hordes of people on the ground below, and hear shouts from them. The closer they came to earth the better they began to feel about their venture. For, amidst the excitement of seeing the people, there was a sign that read "WELCOME!" They knew they were free!

The Cost of Freedom

Your need for freedom may not be physical, but whether it is psychological or spiritual, it is no less real. And it will cost you something to be free! Your ability to break loose depends largely on your willingness to do so. To make that move toward cutting the barriers involves a degree of danger, a chance that not all people are willing to take. What are some of those risks?

1. *There is always the possibility of failure.* Because of this, some women never make an attempt toward personal freedom.

Was not this also the problem of the man in the Gospels who was given one talent? The one-talent man failed to use what was given him for fear of losing it, while the two-talent and five-talent men boldly invested their monies (Matthew 25). There he was, the one-talenter, bound with the haunting possibility of not being able to produce, so he did nothing! He was soon to fall into bondage by his own level of mediocrity. The talent which had been given him was for the sole purpose of being used. The gift was measured according to his ability to use it. Each of the persons in the story was a benefactor according to capability. It was not until the merchant had returned to collect the profits from his investments that the one-talent man realized his mistake.

We, like him, often fail to consider that God never measures success for us by the accomplishments of other people. If we are going to find freedom from the fear of failure, we must learn that a) we must take the first step toward being free by giving back to God that which He has given us (this often means that we will do so at great risk); b) once we have dared surrender the meager ability we have, it then becomes God's responsibility to multiply it; c) because God is fair, He never demands more of us than we can give (His level of acceptance is based upon His understanding of what we are capable of giving); and d) what we may be lacking as individuals He will make up in our lives (provided that we are willing to take that initial step away from failure).

It is encouraging to know that God views us differently from the way we see ourselves, or even as others see us. The economy of His just dealings can be seen through this simple formula, as it pertains to both those who received the talents and to us:

$$5 + 5 = 10$$
$$2 + 2 = 4 + \text{Jesus} = 10$$

If the man who was given only one talent had chosen to use it, as did the others, his rewards would have been equal to theirs. For, whatever deficit or lack in our lives, Christ steps in to make up that difference. The one talent would have worked on the same basis:

$$1 + 1 = 2 + \text{Jesus} = 10$$

Once we have given what we have to Christ, allowing Him to add what we don't have, we come into a realm of spiritual and psychological freedom. 2. *Not only is the risk of failure involved in our attempts for freedom, but there is the demand for self-abandonment to the Person of Jesus Christ.* Doing this brings us into an ongoing freedom as we allow His restorative nature to work in our behalf. Note the words of Jesus while speaking to His disciples:

Anyone who keeps his life for himself
shall lose it; and anyone who loses his life
for me shall find it again (Matthew 16:25).

The act of abandonment is not always easy. In fact,

those outside the kingdom can hardly understand its principles. Even those of us who are Christians often find ourselves struggling with this point. A college professor once talked with me about this aspect of faith. He couldn't see the reasonableness of surrendering his own will to God's.

> Why is it necessary to submit your will, your total self? I would like to be a Christian, but the idea of turning my will over to God is something I cannot accept.

What he failed to understand was that Christ did not stop at asking us to lose ourselves, but said more: "...shall find it again." The finding process is one based upon the essentiality of giving, a voluntary act of surrender—an act that also places God in a position of responsibility toward us.

3. *The other risk for your consideration is the possibility of success.* On the surface you might wonder, *Why would success be a risk?* There are many risk factors involved in striking out to find psychological freedom. For one thing, some of us cannot visualize ourselves as successful persons, not even with the help of God. Because of this kind of psychological/spiritual bondage we hold onto our hangups like a security blanket. On the other hand, success may be something we ourselves work toward but find difficult to accept in other people. Author and consultant Marilyn Machlowitz, in an interview with Elizabeth Mehren of the *Los Angeles Times* (September 5, 1984), talked about this problem as it especially relates to us as women:

> We desire it [success] for ourselves and

detest it in others. We may actively seek
it and yet passively avoid it; success arouses
fears and feelings regardless of the age it
is attained.

Some of us are simply not conditioned for success
because we dare not take the risk! To do so involves
a personal investment in ourselves. Besides, we are
constantly being reinforced by someone who predicts
failure for us. Once we have broken out from a level
of mediocrity, away from the norm, some people will
be uncomfortable in our presence. We know that, and
it can be a deterrent to our efforts! The threat we pose
accentuates the insecurities of other people, making
us vulnerable to their negative feedback. We have all
experienced those reactions at some time in our lives.
I remember once when a charming young lady (at
least I thought she was at first) came up to the platform
where I had just finished speaking and asked:

Why do you want to write a book? You
mentioned in the session that you were
working on a manuscript. In my opinion,
you have nothing to say that would be
worthwhile for putting in print.

Needless to say, I was taken aback. There were
moments when I felt that the risk was too great to
take, and what if it never happened? However, if that
same woman were to go through my files today and
see the countless number of letters from women over-
seas and at home who have been helped by the book
(*Be the Woman You Want to Be*), the success would
be threatening to her. You see, the fact remains that
while I may not consider myself a success, other

people might. The manner in which they perceive me merits some consideration. It simply means that you and I take a risk when we dare to take one step in a forward direction.

If you are growing, breaking loose from the psychological/spiritual bindings of your past, you are a success whether you feel like one or not, even when others don't treat you as if you were. While working on the beforementioned book I ran into another problem. The first publishing firm to whom the material was submitted gave me an almost-positive "yes" to accept it. But after having it near completion, the familiar rejection slip came to me by mail. There I was, remembering what the woman in Reno had told me. *Was she right?* I asked myself. A feeling of embarrassment swept over me; disappointed and brokenhearted, I fell on my knees and began sobbing. I wondered, *Had I tried doing something for which I was totally unqualified? How could I face my husband and children and tell them that my manuscript wasn't good enough for publication? Was it really true that I had nothing to give?*

Sitting there on the floor in our family room, I waited for my emotions to catch up with my intellect. As I lingered there alone, sifting through my thoughts, a surge of peace invaded my thinking process. In my heart I knew that this had to be given to God. If I failed, He would be the final Judge on the matter. What a reassuring release to feel, and to know, that no woman ever makes a failure who dares to give to God what she has! And I knew I had done that. It was as if the Lord had reminded me of that truth. Getting up from the floor and accepting life with its disappointments and joys had become a liberating experience for me. I had learned the art of self-abandonment to a cause that was higher than my ego and pride. Not long after that time Harvest House Publishers had the book on the market, and sales were going very well.

The problem with which you are struggling may not be a spiritual one (such as mine) or possible physical bondage (from which the Hutyra family fled), but it is nonetheless real. You may feel strapped to a cargo basket, being catapulted through the air, not knowing where you are going to land—but hang in there! Whatever the difficulty with which you are struggling at this moment, God will maneuver you through the maze. He will enable you to cut the ropes of personal bondage.

The most important thing is to give what you have to God, leave the results to Him, and let Him lead you. You must be willing to live with the choices you make and to take personal responsibility when those choices are not the best ones.

Point of Action

1. Carefully consider any deterrent you feel is keeping you from spiritual/psychological freedom.

2. Ask yourself: Is this something which has recently surfaced in my life, and how do I approach it from a balanced biblical perspective?

3. Consider all the alternate choices you might have:

PRO   **CON**

4. Where might the choices lead? If you choose either, will your ultimate relationship to Jesus Christ be strengthened by the decision?

5. Think about the motive that is driving you toward freedom. Is it a selfish one? Morally, does it coincide with your personal convictions of right and wrong?

Read 2 Samuel 11—12. Did David's choice bring him freedom?

THERE ARE MANY WAYS IN WHICH OUR ATTI-
TUDES TOWARD FREEDOM HAVE CHANGED.
WHEN WE CONSIDER OUR FREEDOM TO
BREAK GOD'S COMMANDMENTS, THE FACT
BECOMES EVEN MORE EVIDENT.

Chapter 8

What Does Freedom Mean to You?

Today's woman is asking for more than any other woman in the history of the world. She seeks to be both free and liberated—free enough to do her own thing, but with societal laws to protect her while doing it. This kind of attitude has reduced the sacred things of life to commonplace, or no place, in our value systems. These are days when there are few clear-cut absolutes. "Whatever seems right in your own eyes" has become the credo of this generation, and it is being done under the banner of personal freedom!

Those persons who have dared to speak out against what they consider infringements of their personal Christian convictions are labeled as offenders of the law. The media often depicts them as polyester-clad matrons with the mental acumen of an insane person. It would appear, from what we are now seeing, that Christians are considered as being the "root of all evil."

Those who propagate the idea of "doing what comes naturally" as an acceptable mode of behavior often consider those persons on the other end of the spectrum as rabble-rousers, to be blamed for any political backlash on those issues.

This approach of transferred blame is one that goes back into history. One of the earliest accounts of this is found in the example of Elijah, an Old Testament prophet of King Ahab's time. When Ahab reigned as King of Israel, he rebuilt worship centers that were dedicated to the gods of Baal. The king was so insecure in his own relationship toward the true God that he had to take direction from 400 prophets of Belial with whom he had surrounded himself.

Then, after having broken every command of God concerning the tearing down of idolatry worship, Ahad found the nation over which he reigned in a great dearth. There was famine throughout the land, a condition caused by the people's transgressions against the known commandments of God. But when the prophet Elijah came on the scene, it was he who was blamed for all the trouble!

Elijah, fearful for his safety, was in hiding when the Lord spoke to him. The prophet was instructed to go to the king and make his whereabouts known. Fearful for his life, the man of God hesitated before being reassured that the Lord's presence would go before him. One would think that by this time, with a nation so near starvation and looking for water that could scarcely be found, the ruler of that nation would welcome the appearance of the prophet.

Not so!

Instead of asking for the prophet's help, Ahab's first words to Elijah were: "So it's you, is it?—the man who brought this disaster upon Israel!" (1 Kings 18:17).

We need only look around us to understand that the same posture exists today. Not only so, but this shift in personal responsibility has also brought about a general change in attitude concerning biblical standards of behavior.

Changing Attitudes

There are many ways in which our attitudes about freedom have changed. When we consider our freedom to break the Ten Commandments without any troubling of conscience, this becomes more evident. Look at the commandment "Thou shall not commit adultery" and observe what is now taking place. We have only to remember that a decade ago pornography (a form of adultery) was banned in almost every state. Now the national consensus has begun to make a flip-flop; often those who wish to ban the illicit material have become the criminals! The purveyors are set free while those in opposition are made to be the culprits.

What once began as rights of privacy has evolved into a public-action force. Sex is commercialized until we are inundated with its images. You can hardly watch television or read the newspapers (to say nothing of going to a theater) without being bombarded with scenes that tear at the heart of the believer. Situation comedies make evangelical Christians the brunt of their slapstick antics. No other minority group in our nation is maligned more than are the fundamentalists. If any other segment of society was treated in this matter a cry would go up that would shake the political world.

We are not only the objects of bad intent, but are victimized by the manner in which preferential lifestyles are encouraged. Even our children are caught in the cross-pull of the new freedom movements. Our kids can pick up the telephone and hear the most explicit of conversations about sex. Everywhere we look we can see the effect of this "battle of the minds." Just recently I picked up an insert from a local newspaper television listing which read, "A feast of adultery, violence and sex!" This was the header announcing a program that was to be aired that week.

Is This Freedom?

To oppose such blatant openness to violence and sex is to be branded as enemies of the cause of freedom. The libertarians call themselves "Friends of the Woman" and consider those of us from a Christian background as being deceptive in our intent. They insist that we wish to keep women under some kind of chauvinistic slavery.

What a reversal of attitudes!

Where once the value systems of America's growing populace were determined largely by biblical concepts, they are now based on human reasoning. Humanistic thought has taught our children they descended from apes, allowing them to grow up with an undisciplined freedom unparalleled by that of any other time. In some cases we have lived to see the day when human rights have taken precedence over life itself, and this is all being done under the high-flying banner of freedom.

It was this kind of thinking that produced a generation of youth who have made heroes out of drug addicts, are pushing for the legalization of prostitution, and are making a mockery of the marriage vows. One woman from the radical left clearly defined her position while being interviewed on television. She talked about what she called "mystification as being oppression."

What did she mean?

First, her statement implied that women are not free until the mystery of sex has been fully explored. Second, she meant that to keep such things as our marriages sacred was to bring ourselves under oppression. Because of the commonplace acceptance of "evil being good," society has begun to accept it as such. The law of attrition is at work. Having been exposed to something long enough, we find it easier to accept. Once enough people begin to accept a particular practice, they tend to pass laws that will protect themselves while doing it. Somehow even Christians have difficulty in sorting these things out. In some cases we have begun to feel that if something is being sanctioned by the government, it is also acceptable in the eyes of God.

These attitudinal changes are most evident in relation to the Sixth Commandment ("Thou shalt not kill"). The approach to life has been altered to respect the privileges of promiscuity. The "human rights" that are flaunted before us have also given us the right to kill, through abortion, over one million babies annually. While doing so, we are represented by those who wave the banner beneath the sanctions of the Supreme Court.

On that fateful day in January 1973 when abortion on demand was made a mandate, many church women never blinked a religious eyelash in protest. Still, we have looked with horror and listened with shock at the news media giving accounts of thousands of aborted fetuses being wrapped in plastic bags and thrown into garbage cans. If this had been animal carcasses instead, the act would have incurred "the wrath of the gods" upon the offenders. What a tragedy when our bodies, as women, become nothing more than the objects of free-wheeling sex, and our selfish desire for freedom is considered the criterion for life!

From Freedom to Myth

Those promised freedoms have become the vehicle which has carried the twentieth-century woman into a different kind of bondage. The freedom has become a myth! The thing once believed to be liberating has brought women into a kind of sexual exploitation and moral degradation. No one suspected that this would happen—that we women would become victims of the very thing that was to have brought us freedom. We were told that free expression would eliminate violence. Many well-meaning persons bought the idea and argued for its merits. We were (and are) encouraged to help legalize prostitution because we are told that it will create happier marriages, reduce the amount of venereal disease, and provide us safe alternatives. This naive notion on the part of some has resulted in making men less sensitive to the "caring needs" of women.

Dr. Neil Malamuth, Professor of Sociology at UCLA, did a recent study. It was his opinion, after having interviewed a group of men, that they tended to trivialize rape and see aggression toward women as acceptable behavior in this society. Masochism (abnormal sexual passion characterized by pleasure in being abused by one's associate or partner) is encouraged by many of the rock-singing groups. Their lyrics are full of it. In 1976 the Rolling Stones made the most blatant attempt at commercializing this sadistic ritual. They posted a billboard on a prominent street in Los Angeles which read "I'm Black and Blue from the Rolling Stones and I Love it." Soon a plethora of graphic pictures showing women in chains and being beaten hit the market. Such record covers filled the music stands, and women became the victims of distorted minds.

Only two years after this sign appeared on a major thoroughfare, a men's magazine jumped on the escalator of downward trends. The cover page of this well-known periodical depicted a woman's nude half-body, with her upper torso and legs in the air. The other portion of her anatomy was shown being ground up like hamburger, pulverized into shreds.

These so-called freedoms are more than a myth— they have become a nightmare. We, the women, have become pawns of the sexually perverted mind. Even some on the liberated front have begun to take a stand against such abuse. Some who were once participants in X-rated movies are now giving second thoughts to what is happening. One young actress who starred in an early movie rated X dared to speak out against this form of brutality. She was being interviewed on television and told how she felt about being a part of the film. Now, a few years older and wiser, the actress told her listening audience, "What you thought you saw happening and what was appearing to be a pleasurable experience was not so at all. What you actually saw was my being used, as if raped."

Whether she spoke in actuality or as a symbol of speech I cannot say. However, she made it perfectly clear that what the viewing audience thought they saw was not true. It was only a facade of pleasure—a myth of happiness!

Another point concerning all of these promised mythical freedoms deals with what was intended to be sex education in our schools. I am not arguing here whether or not it is needed. But it is worth considering what the program has deteriorated into, at least in some cases. When the curriculum was initiated, its merits were praised as being a value-free approach to learning. Yet when President Reagan suggested that the curriculum include abstention and chastity as alternatives for youth, he was ridiculed.

All this has brought us to the point of looking into our freedom, and of making sure that all people are actually free—free to follow not only our dreams but to follow Christ, who makes us truly free!

Point of Action

1. Define in 25 words or less what twentieth-century freedom means to you personally.

2. Define what you feel is spiritual freedom.

3. How do the above affect your psychological freedom?

4. What did Jesus mean by John 8:31-38?

5. Can the above verses of Scripture be applied to daily living? If so, how?

IF IT IS TRUE THAT WE ARE WHAT WE EAT, IT
IS ALSO TRUE THAT WE ARE THE PRODUCTS
OF OUR LIFE'S CHOICES.

Chapter 9

Your Responsibility and Choices

Each generation of women, since the beginning of
time, has been in hot pursuit of personal freedom.
Historically, freedom for the woman has carried a
different meaning with each successive generation.
Not only so, but women have had to cope and live
within the confines of the sociological definitions of
those cultural freedoms. The rules of her societal
behavior, as related to freedom, were changing within
the mores of her geographical surroundings. Women's
personal liberties have often had to do with her role
in society. In most cases the role was an assigned one,
keeping her in the home. Her voting rights were
limited and she was not considered political
bait...until now!

Many of the major issues of our recent political elections were centered around women's rights. We women, while working in our homes and employed on jobs, watched as our votes were being courted by the nation's candidates. Never has there been a presidential election when gender became such a political factor. Women have come a long way in their search for freedom, and there are varied opinions as to how those choices of newfound freedom are affecting the home and family.

Prior to the 1940's, woman's place in society was considered as being strictly in the home. Today's woman has a different role. She is relatively free to pursue any vocation she chooses, whether a mother rocking her newborn baby or a medical doctor orbiting the earth in a spaceship. Since her role is no longer destined to be in the home, her options of freedom are varied. With these options comes a greater sense of responsibility. It is highly possible that she can abuse those freedoms, making it difficult for future generations. She is much like a traveler going into a foreign country, experiencing the unknown cultures of a different society. Because of this she dare not accept her freedom as a license to disregard the God-ordained privileges that are hers.

Throughout the past few years we have heard words coming from our European neighbors calling us "ugly Americans." Why? Could it be that those who were representing us abroad misused their rights of travel? Did they fail to live up to the ambassadorial responsibilities of those privileges?

We as women need only observe the breakdown in the family units to understand that something has gone awry in our society. That strong force, the place where we went for support—our homes—is now being torn apart. The mobile society in which we live has replaced the once-secure feeling of the "old homestead." During World War II there was a great migration away from our homes. Families were uprooted as uncles, brothers, sweethearts, and husbands went away to fight in the war. Sisters, aunts, or other relatives joined the WAC's WAVE's, USO, and other branches of the armed service. Young men who had helped work our farms and run our city governments were drafted before even understanding the nature of combat. Everywhere, in every post office in America, was Uncle Sam pointing his finger and saying, "Uncle Sam Needs You!"

Throughout the Midwest and across the farmlands of America, people set out to answer his challenge. Homes were sold; cattle, livestock, and farm equipment were auctioned off to the highest bidder. Couples whose forebears had lived and died on those farms (having never traveled more than 50 miles from their birthplace) loaded their clothes, mattresses, and camping stoves onto beat-up automobiles and headed for the big city.

Many women who had never before been employed outside their homes found jobs in the shipyards. Big money and fast bucks lured them! Pulling on overalls and tying their hair in bandannas, they began riveting their way into America's work force. Their motives were not questioned because what they were doing was being done in the name of freedom. This was the first time a woman from a traditional background of society could feel free to leave her children in a day center or with a babysitter. Prior to that time only a minority of women had pursued careers outside the home. Women bought war bonds from monies earned. They invested monthly checks being mailed them from their men in the military services, and they developed a new and growing independence.

Changing Freedoms

When the war ended, the husbands and sweethearts returned, but there was trouble on the homefront. The families they had left were no longer securely nestled on properties once owned by their parents. Mom and Dad were uprooted and deposited in crackerbox houses built to accommodate the rapidly growing city population. Discharged servicemen found themselves trying to be assimilated back into the workforce or hoping to reestablish their families on the old homeplace. Uncle Sam had by this time finished needing the women to toil in factories. He was finished with them, but they were not through with Uncle Sam!

Within a decade the "baby boom" hit as fathers came home and young soldiers found wives. The nation's economy dropped, shipyards began closing, and Army bases shut down. There were only a few options left for the returning GI's. Many of them entered school on the government's Bill of Rights. Mothers and wives went back to work, helping supplement the family income. Changed environmental surroundings, war nerves, and social adjustments produced more stress than some couples could cope with. As a result of many changes, we experienced a soaring divorce rate, one that was soon to reach a proportion of one out of three marriages!

The sacred vows of marriage were being litigated in the civil courts of our nation. Once the contractual agreement was arbitrated by a judge, the contract could be easily broken. Whatever properties the couple might have acquired was divided by law. Children born to them became viewed as legal property and treated much the same. In order to accommodate our newly acquired married status, it became increasingly necessary to enact civil laws that would expedite the judicial system. Judges, already overloaded with paperwork, began recommending methods that would assist them in their work. Out of this growing concern the no-fault dissolution laws came into effect.

Throughout the years that followed we have observed an almost complete epidemic of failure in the home and family. War-boom babies began growing up but had few roots and lacked a sense of belonging. Families were broken, fragmented, torn apart. In many cases, society was oblivious to their needs. The church was in its theological trenches, singing "Hold the Fort" while its nation's youth were begging for identification with a cause to which they could relate. With homes broken into pieces, a government working to get its people back to normality, and the church's ecclesiastical blindness, we lost a generation of young people.

It is a commonly accepted fact that once a traditional concept has been destroyed there will be something to take its place! In this case drugs, the occult, and meditation stepped in to fill the void. By means of transcendental meditation, youth were encouraged to get in touch with their better selves and make contact with a higher order. Drugs and communal living gave them a sense of belonging. No sooner had these teenagers gone out on their own than we began to see their marks upon society. Because they had no foundation within the God-given

establishments of home, church, and state, they set
out to destroy these institutions. They moved into
communes, advocated open sex, and became flower
children singing songs about love. The spiritual
condition of our nation was approaching that of
Israel's when the psalmist asked:

> If the foundations be destroyed, what
> can the righteous do? (Psalm 11:3 KJV).

The Living Bible gives these words an even stronger
meaning:

> The wicked have strung their bows,
> drawn arrows tight against their bows, and
> aimed from ambush at the people of God.
> Law and order have collapsed (Psalm
> 11:2,3).

While our nation's disoriented youth roamed the
streets or sat in fields strumming guitars and singing,
they were making inquiries about life, death, and
political issues. Those unanswered queries became
the lighted torches which burned our schools,
churches, and public buildings. Our choices, and
theirs, were being made in the name of freedom.

It was during this decade that I was taking a
sociology class on one of the campuses in Los
Angeles. Each session was filled with rabid hostilities
voiced by students. We were told each week where
the next "burn" was being planned, and what areas
of the city would next go up in smoke.

Freedom's Choices

Freedom had brought with it some choices, and
the winds of philosophical change were blowing upon

us from every direction. Young families were being influenced by the principles of child rearing as taught in Dr. Spock's book. "Spockism" advocated permissiveness, favoring the psychological freedom of the growing child. Out of this melee of disorder, broken homes, and children without parents (having no roots and little discipline) we produced two generations of youth. These are young people whose value systems have moved us from Christian traditionalism to the philosophical far left.

From this disconcerting background today's woman is struggling between the old and the new concepts of freedom. She is setting out to find herself, to experience a feeling of independence, as she heads into a concrete jungle of the unknown. She is seeking, sometimes unknowingly, to have the best of two worlds.

When the women's liberation movement first began, it had an almost insidious attitude toward the woman in the home. Motherhood, for these people, was nothing more than an option that could be delayed, or never experienced, until conditions were right. A woman was not considered fulfilled if she chose to marry, remain home, and raise a family. That feeling has been modified, at least on the surface, as single women are encouraged to bear children without a permanent marriage partner.

What started as a breath of wind has now become a full-blown tornado. It is one that is tearing its way into every fabric of our lives. Cyndi Lauper, a well-known rock star and sex symbol of the '80's, has openly avowed her distaste for the God-given establishments, calling them the greatest deterrents to a woman's freedom. On the surface we might think her position to be an isolated one, but we have only to look around us to see clergymen, politicians, and the media defend the same rationale.

When you consider that those young persons who once advocated violence are now integrated into the fabric of our society, setting many of the ground rules for personal behavior, you can better understand what is happening. Where are those persons now? They are politicians, corporate chairpersons, television producers, lawyers, and bankers. They represent every vocation of life. About the only visible change is that many of them have replaced the hippie look with a clean-shaven appearance. Their once-ragged clothes, a symbol of their past, have been exchanged for a Madison Avenue suit or designer dress. It is from this group that much of the decision-making of American philosophy is being shaped. While their appearance may be changed, their credo is much the same. Because of this bombardment of conflicting ideology, we as women are facing decisions much more difficult than those known by any previous generation of women in our country. Not only so, but future generations will be affected by the decisions and choices we are now making.

Our Responsibility

We will have to take the responsibility for our choices. Someone once said, "Each generation of people gets the youth they deserve." We are responsible not only for our own actions but also for understanding the actions of other people as well. Throwing off restraints may seem good for the moment, but what are the end results? That is the question each woman must ask herself.

A young woman who sat sobbing in our office a

few years ago had not stopped to consider the effect that her choice was going to make upon her future life. Luanna was caught up in her personal need for freedom.

> My parents were strict, at times too strict. The main aim of my teenage years was to get old enough to leave home. Being raised in church (and once having a close personal relationship with Jesus Christ) did not keep me from pursuing my own selfish desires. Somehow I found myself putting my Christian convictions on hold while I set out to find the freedom I was determined to get.
>
> After a brief love affair I became pregnant by a man I thought I loved. We didn't bother to get married because our love relationship was supposed to have been greater than a piece of paper (that's what we called it). As I embarked on my free-living lifestyle, I was idealistic, feeling that my relationship with this man would continue forever. But it didn't. Left with a baby to support and broken down in health, I found myself coming to my senses and calling again upon God.

This sort of problem is facing every young person today. The question of morality is becoming broader and broader as promiscuous lifestyles are encouraged. The subliminal conditioning process facing us today was unheard of in other eras. Marketing experts are working overtime to present products describing sex as a normal recreational pastime experience without the inconvenience of marriage sanctions. Commercials depict subtle but mind-boggling techniques as almost-nude women are shown in lightning-quick movements parading in the background. What is all of this saying to us?

Does it mean that our teenagers are expected to accept nudity as the norm? What about these choices? Are we not already reaping some of those decisions made earlier? Marilyn Russell Bittle, President of the California Teachers Association, wrote in the *Los Angeles Times* on December 18, 1984, giving the following 1983 statistics:

* 2 million cases of child abuse in the U.S. in 1983.
* 5000 youngsters die annually from brutality.
* One child is murdered every two hours of the day, 365 days of the year.

In the August 8, 1982, edition of *Parade* magazine appeared an article entitled "Who Can Resist Natassia?" In one corner of the same page is a picture of the actress, showing her nude body with a snake stretched between her legs for the length of her body. "First, we tried making the picture with clothes, which didn't work. It was hard to get the snake positioned properly," states the actress. When that same photo appeared in *Vogue* magazine, the religious world was shocked. What many people did not know was that it had become (or was rapidly becoming) the number one poster of the time, appearing on billboards as well as in print. Who is this actress, who was barely out of her teens when she posed for the poster? She is a sex symbol of the '80's.

Kinski recalls her home life as being a parody: family breakups, destruction of the house, violent fights followed by tears, and times of family reconciliations. Being the child of divorced parents, her acting career began at the early age of 13, and she became Roman Polanski's lover at age 15.

Personal Accountability

We are morally responsible for our choices in life!

1. *With every privilege there is a responsibility toward self-discipline.* Discipline (not a word that is popular among us these days!) is the track upon which freedom's train must run. Once the locomotive of life moves off the restricted path of personal restraint, chaos becomes inevitable and we are headed for psychological wreckage. Hear the words of Solomon, the wise king, who confessed his former folly by saying in Ecclesiastes chapter 2:

> Anything I wanted, I took, and did not restrain myself (v. 10).
>
> As I looked at everything I had tried, it was useless, a chasing of the wind (v.11).

2. *With every responsibility there are choices comparable to the task.* Since we are responsible to be our brother's keeper, those choices are measured accordingly. True freedom is that which seeks not only to be free oneself, but to see that others are free as well.

3. *With every choice is a personal accountability to God.* Opportunity and accountability are closely related throughout the Scriptures. Take, for instance,

the parable of the ten virgins (Matthew 25:1-13). The five foolish virgins were given opportunities equal to those of the five wise ones. The first five failed to grasp their moment of opportunity, yet they were personally accountable to the bridegroom for having made no provisions to meet him.

While there is within each one of us as women that need for self-fulfillment, let us not forget that with today's opportunities there are also responsibilities. The need for freedom always assumes that there are barriers, and these are the strongholds of prisondom that God seeks to break through in our lives, bringing us personal freedom!

Point of Action

1. How far can the Christian woman go in pursuit of her personal freedom? Does the Bible place any restraints on her freedom?

2. Does God permit us to break His biblical commands for the sake of our personal rights of freedom?

3. What part do our relationships with other people have in our search for freedom and fulfillment?

Read the model prayer given in Matthew 6:9-13. Do you feel that this prayer is applicable to your needs of personal freedom? If so, how?

STEP IV

FREEDOM:
IT'S WORTH IT!

Fear not, for I am with you. Do not be
dismayed. I am your God. I will strengthen
you; I will help you; I will uphold you with
my victorious right hand.

Isaiah 41:10

> NO MATTER HOW INNOCENT A NEGATIVE WORD MAY APPEAR, ONCE THE WORD IS SPOKEN IT BECOMES PART OF YOU AND IS STORED IN THE COMPUTER OF YOUR SUBCONSCIOUS MIND.

Chapter 10

Building Your Inner Resources

Within each of us are two untapped wellsprings from which we may draw strength. One is outside ourselves and the other is self-contained. From the earliest point of childhood until now we have been placing deposits in those reserves. A trove of treasures is being stored in the subconscious mind and lies buried there. Through a volitional act of our will we choose what we wish to deposit. Unfortunately, that ability to choose is often taken for granted. We often do not filter the good things from the bad.

No matter how innocent a negative thought may appear, once spoken it goes on the mind's computer. A movie laced with obscenity may seem to be only a fleeting thought, never to be remembered again.

Not so! Once we have chosen to see something with our eyes and hear it with our ears, it becomes part of us. Every incident is recorded on the tablet of our minds. Like it or not, once placed there it will resurface. There will be a time when, faced with a decision, the memory button of your mind's computer will bring the scene back to you. Eventually, when finding yourself in a similar situation, it will then be much easier to respond on the level of negative conditioning. It is from this inner resource that we draw our emotional impulses. No wonder we are told, "As we think we become."

Since life holds no degree of predictability, we live most of the time between a dichotomy of laughter and tears, chaos and bliss. We may even begin to feel that we are walking a tightrope, doing a balancing act on a precipice, with the emotional self hanging in the balance. Each day brings its share of new experiences, and we must cope accordingly.

About the time everything in life seems under control, something happens: One of the kids' schoolteachers calls, saying, "Your son is ill; can you come and get him?" You get in the car, only to discover that it won't start. The phone rings, and it's Father. "Could you come and bring me the extra set of keys? I've just locked myself out of the office." How we respond during these times depends largely upon our ability to draw from the wellspring of positive thoughts. If the previous input has been negative, we will find it difficult to get from point A to B. There is a proneness toward viewing the situation as a whole rather than as a segment in life. Not being able to properly evaluate the frictional incidents of life causes them to grind away at us like sandpaper. So, in order to give ourselves some semblance of balance, we resort to other forms of negative problem-solving.

1. We build walls, closing other people away from us.
2. We gulp down medication to keep our physical bodies going.
3. We attack everyone around us because we feel that we have been attacked ourselves.
4. We get sick with psychosomatic illnesses as our bodies try to adjust to the strain.
5. We get bitter toward God, feeling that life is unfair to us, that He has destined us to a life of tragedy.

Few of us fail to consider why we are responding this way, so we cut ourselves off from two main resources of strength: our friends and our God.

Drawing from the Well of Friendship

Your friends are the most valuable resource you can accumulate. When life is dealing you what you think is an unfair blow, friends can help you through it. I never understood the importance of this more than when a friend once sensed my need.

We were living in California's San Joaquin Valley. During late winter that area of the state is often blanketed with thick layers of fog. At this time the sun had not shown its face for several days. Everything around me was gloomy! The situation of my life was worsened because of my being stricken with the flu bug. I was trapped in by the fog and my self-image was low (from a feeling of rejection for having missed a family gathering).

This seemed to be a very convenient time to have a good cry. Being in the midst of a fever recovery, and being alone in the house, I had the opportunity for a "pity party." With a big box of Kleenex in hand, I propped myself up in Claude's comfortable chair and let the tears begin to flow. I had just begun enjoying my dilemma when the doorbell rang. (Have you ever noticed how it happens every time?) There I was, feeling so depressed that it felt good to be depressed, yet I knew I had to answer the door. I dragged my body to the front of the house and slowly opened the door.

"Who is it?"

"Are you Ruthe White?" (That day I would liked to have been anyone other than myself!)

"Yes."

I pulled the door open a little wider and stood breathless as a man's hand pushed through the entry. For a moment I was frightened by what appeared to be an intrusion of my privacy. Instead, the person handed me a dozen red carnations. They were beautiful, with long stems, and arranged in an elegant container. Attached to the bouquet was a note which read:

I love you.
A friend.

No name was signed. I set the flowers on the dining room table and headed for the family room. No, I didn't need the tissues any longer, for I was saying to myself, *I am loved, someone in this city loves me!* The crying session was ended. A friend had cared enough to allow me to draw from her resource of strength that day. I wondered who had given me the carnations, to later discover that they had been sent by Judy Neill, a member of my young married's Christian Living Class.

These are the moments that bring rewards—these unexpected times when God places friends in our lives to strengthen and help us. Why? Because we all hurt, we all feel, and we all need support outside ourselves. Thoreau once said, "The mass of men lead lives of quiet desperation." William Marston, a psychologist, once asked 300 people the question, "What do you live for?" Nine persons out of ten replied that they were waiting for something good to happen to them. They were "marking time," hoping for some windfall, a different house, a win in the sweepstakes, or something else. Rather than depositing their energies into *today*, their lives were centered around the unexpected bliss of an unknown future.

Few of us have learned the secret of what the French call "le petit bonhuer"—the little happiness—that comes into our daily lives. We are conditioned to expect the wins, the accolades, the compliments, the affirmations, upon which we feed. But when our feet have to touch base with reality, there is no reserve of personal strength from which to draw. Life often becomes little more than a dreaded fear as we pull against the present and deplete our physical and spiritual energies. Jesus warned us about this when He said:

> Don't be anxious about tomorrow. God will take care of your tomorrow too. Live one day at a time (Matthew 6:34).

This becomes the "daily bread" concept of our resource. When we are always in search of the tomorrows we miss the blessings of today, overlooking the need to build friendships and interpersonal relationships. To do this is to dam up the wellspring of our own potential strengths. We also stop the flow of God's blessings as they come from His hand, and from the hands of others. No one denies that there are moments when we are temporarily thrown off-balance, needing to touch base with reality. The point is not "Do we have those times?" but "How do we cope with them?" There are occasions when friends cannot help us—only God.

Drawing from God's Resources

Our greatest strength is not found in friends alone, as helpful as they may be. The final and ultimate power is found in Christ. Jesus, in conversing with His disciples, made one thing clear: *Now you are my friends* (John 15:15).

Let us never forget that when our spiritual legs are too weak to bear us up, we have a friend in Him. We can find the help needed if we rely upon the strong arm of the Lord.

> He himself gives life and breath to every-
> thing, and satisfies every need there is (Acts
> 17:25).

However difficult it may be to trust God during the troubled moments, you will find it much easier if you have built a trusting relationship with Him. Since life is a daily adventure, our relationship with Him should be an ongoing one. God is not to be used merely as a fire escape, one we jump onto when caught in the heat of life's fires. He is much more than that! Unless we allow God to become the resource center, we may find ourselves groping for the escape hatch.

Yes, God has promised to never leave us or forsake us, but to really *know* God is to have a personal relationship with Him. If we acquaint ourselves with the reality of who He is, it will be much easier to lean upon Him in times of trouble. Building this kind of trust involves a process of depositing His thoughts, His words, and His principles in the computer of our daily lives. Once we learn the secret of doing so, we find Him bringing joy and adding strength in our times of personal weakness.

These hidden resources may never surface until we reach a point of need. Most importantly, there is a principle of life that can be self-sustaining. If we deposit the right things into our inner self, they will be there. The "Law of Life" affirms this principle. I never realized this more than when our grandson Koby was born. He was two months premature, and a valve failed to close at birth. There he was with all the complications that usually follow such a condition: pneumonia and hyaline membrane. He was not expected to survive. Deanna, our daughter and his mother, tells how she struggled, knowing that God was her only resource:

> I was too physically weak from having given birth to fight what appeared to be the inevitable. My emotional and spiritual energy were depleted. There I lay in the silence of early morning, viewing life through a shroud of death. Already the nurses had informed us of Koby's condition as being highly critical. He was not expected to live more than a few hours. Beside my bed was a tiny rosebud that someone had placed there. As I looked at it, still closed, trying

to unfold in the morning sunlight, I began to weep. Somehow I imagined the rose blossom a picture of my tiny child fighting for survival, wanting to live as he was battling the odds. While there observing the beauty of the flower, my heart cried out:

"God, Koby is my child by birth, but Yours through conception. I feel so helpless: There is nothing more that can be done; the doctors and nurses are working around the clock. Lord, I know You love him more than I could ever learn to, so You can understand why I want him to live. I want to take him into my bosom, nurse him, feel his tiny heartbeat next to mine, and to nurture him. But, God, should You choose to take this child, I am willing to give him to You. Whatever You do, if You take him or leave him, my love for You will always remain the same."

Deanna knew at that very moment that her strength for survival rested in the Lord. She said, "I felt God's strength released in me."

Koby pulled through the ordeal. The valve closed on its own while they were en route from Whittier to Huntington Memorial Hospital in Pasadena, where open-heart surgery was scheduled for that day. Three days later he was released and brought home. The child is now eight, active in sports, enrolled in the gifted child program, and functioning on a healthy, normal basis.

While sharing this story in Prescott, Arizona, at a ladies' retreat where I was speaking, a woman came to me with her story:

> My son was born with the same prob-
> lems. Only my child didn't live. God's
> strength was made real to me during the
> loss, and even now I draw from that well
> of resource.

You may be there, depleted, looking for help, not knowing where to turn. When you have done all you can do, there is a source outside yourself. Look inwardly right now and see His workmanship in you. Look outward and don't be afraid to share your hurting moments with a friend who can help you. Most of all, look upward to God, for it is from Him that the flow of strength comes, sweeping you into freedom.

Point of Action

1. Examples of friendships:
   Ruth and Naomi (Ruth 1:16,17)
   Jonathan and David (1 Samuel 18:1-4)

2. How does Proverbs 17:17 affect our relationships?

3. Five points in friendship:

   A. Make friends with persons of all ages, sexes, and social backgrounds.

B. Allow room for other people to be human, to fail, to be themselves.
C. Invest your better self in others.
D. Make your friendship a learning experience.
E. Keep the communication lines open.

4. What obligation do you have toward your mental well-being? Ask:

A. Am I negative in my outlook toward life?
B. Do I generally expect and receive the best from others? If not, why?
C. Can I usually look to the brighter side of things?

5. Do I feed the inner self with positives—good thoughts, good reading material, and good friends? How can I improve?

WE ARE ALL SUBJECT TO THREE KINDS OF
GUILT: GUILT WE IMPOSE UPON OURSELVES,
GUILT WE ALLOW OTHERS TO HEAP UPON US,
AND GUILT OF SIN.

Chapter 11

Resolving Your Guilt

I have billboard-size guilt. There is something about my nature that causes me to
automatically assume responsibility that is
not mine. What can I do to help myself?

These words were coming from a loving, caring
mother who expressed her frustrations to me at the
close of a seminar session. She was honest in her
desire to know and do the right thing. That same
sensitivity toward God and others was driving her to
a point of desperation. Her inability to know when
she had done enough and when to say no are the
same problems that other women face. We often find

it difficult to prioritize our roles, and so we take on the weight of the whole world.

One day the doctor looked at me and said:

> Ruthe, my treatment for you this week is to go home and do nothing—absolutely nothing. I want you to lie down on the floor and rest. Turn off the motors: Don't plan any speaking engagements, committee meetings, or anything else while resting.

I thought to myself, "What a snap!"

Then the physician told me something about myself I didn't want to hear:

> You are trying to do too much. It appears that when you have all you can carry in one arm, you load up the other in order to keep yourself in balance.

His statements threw me a bit out of kilter with all my planned projects for the week. When I tried taking his advice and doing nothing, as he had said, I found it to be one of the most difficult undertakings of my life. Just to stay there on the floor, with music playing, having the mental motors in neutral, was a real effort for me. For years I had been juggling roles between the busy activities of a wife, mother, preacher's wife, teacher, and speaker. There was no way I could stop, as the doctor suggested, and still do all the things I felt needed to be done.

Because of a problem with my immune system, there was no way I could continue the pace that I was presently keeping. Somehow I had to bring my priorities into focus, and no one but I could determine what they were. Deciding those priorities meant that some things would have to be left undone. Taking a pencil and paper in hand and defining my most important roles was helpful. You may want to do the same. Begin with what is most important:

Wife

Mother

Working Woman

Other

Under each category write out what has to be done each day.

Establish the same type of priority listing for each major role you fill.

Role No. 1   **Role No. 2**   **Role No. 3**

Now that you have named those things, put them under the proper role listing, and start working on a schedule allocating time for the most essential things. Investigate the possibility of assigning some of the responsibilities to other members of the family. Combine as many duties as you can, and begin working toward goals to relieve some of the pressures. Start learning your level of strengths and weaknesses. (We all have them!)

Out of this area of role conflicts comes our greatest guilt. The guilty feeling "I am neglecting one thing to do another" develops. Three kinds of guilt should be identified: sin guilt, transferred guilt (imposed upon us by others), and self-imposed guilt. Since self-imposed guilt seems the most difficult with which to cope, let's look at it first.

Self-Imposed Guilt

Imaginary guilt is usually associated with our roles, a break from our traditional past, or a change in our self-identity. The sensitive woman is most vulnerable to this free-floating anxiety. She often tries to be a combination of all the biblical women while being a twentieth-century example of motherhood. Like a puppet on a string, everyone pulls at her. As a mother she is controlled by what she thinks a mother should be. Always trying, but never able to reach her ideal, she gets down on herself, inflicting pain upon herself through guilt.

Transferred Guilt

Much the same as the woman whose schedule is controlled by her imaginary guilt, this woman accepts guilt from others. Like the woman who was struggling with her "billboard-size problem," she takes on everyone else's problems.

Unfortunately, this situation becomes self-perpetuating. As other people observe our willingness to accept, they willingly give. Soon we discover that we are unable to distinguish between who is placing those pressures upon whom.

One lady I know said she felt so guilty because of being overweight that she accepted as her sole responsibility any job that needed to be done. Consequently, everyone around her transferred their workload over to her. Trying to do more and more (and feeling guilty because she couldn't) drove her to a point of physical, mental, and spiritual exhaustion. What was the woman to have done?

1. She had to take responsibility for herself by learning to say no.
2. She had to examine the motives behind what was being done. Was it for acceptance or to prove her worth?
3. She had to decide for herself that she would not accept blame for someone else's hangups.

Sin Guilt

The question of sin guilt is as old as Adam and Eve. However, resolving that issue is as simple as confessing our sin:

> Lord Jesus, I confess my sin and my
> need of You. I know I cannot save myself.
> You, and You alone, can resolve this sin
> guilt in my life. I accept You now and
> believe that, according to 1 John 1:9, if I

confess my sin You will forgive me of all
my sins and cleanse me from all unright-
ousness. Upon the basis of Your Word and
through Your shed blood, I now accept
salvation.

Once this step has been taken, your past sins are
forgiven. But what often happens at this point is that
we are unable to forgive ourselves. Buried within the
subconscious of our minds is the knowledge of all the
sinful things we have done. These often surface at
the least-expected moments, and we allow ourselves
to feel remorse and guilt. It is often easier to think
that God forgives than to be able to forgive ourselves.
Or, since we are unable to be self-forgiving, we doubt
that God will forgive us either.

A vicious merry-go-round of guilt sets in. To make
God love us, we try to work our way toward His
acceptance. Wanting to assuage our feelings of guilt,
we do anything possible to cause others to like us,
feeling guilty when we think they don't.

SELF-PERPETUATING GUILT

GUILT PATTERNS

One of the most freeing experiences of my life was in maturing to the point that I could give people the "right of disliking me." As a minister's wife I wanted to feel loved by the parishioners. Not until I discovered how humanly impossible that was did I rid myself of that guilt. You see, if everyone is supposed to like us, but they don't, we tend to feel responsible for their actions—unless we have learned the freedom of living and letting others live.

We all seek freedom—freedom from our fears, hangups and guilt. We want to be free from any bondage that prevents us from reaching our full potential in life. This is a God-given right. We were not made to be subjects of tyranny. If we can truly seek God first, earnestly desiring that His kingdom be worked out in every facet of our lives, we will know cultural, personal, and spiritual freedom. "If the Son sets you free, you will indeed be free" (John 8:36).

Point of Action

Read 1 John 1:9; Isaiah 43:25; Ephesians 1:7; Hebrews 10:23; Acts 11:9.

WHEN FEAR DOMINATES US, IT BECOMES
BOTH OUR OPPRESSOR AND OUR POSSES-
SOR. WE WILL NEVER KNOW TRUE FREEDOM
UNTIL WE ARE ABLE TO BREAK THE VISELIKE
GRIP OF FEAR.

Chapter 12

Conquering Fear

During my preadolescent years our family's farm-
land adjoined the county cemetery. The community's
burial grounds lay across the ravine and atop a small
knoll about a mile from our house. If we wanted to
travel in a westerly direction (which was the only road
leading to my favorite cousin's place), we had to pass
by the cemetery en route. Sometimes I wanted to play
with my relative so much that I mustered enough
courage to walk the road alone.

To this day I can recall the feel of my rapid heartbeat and the flow of adrenaline that surged through
my body as fear gripped me when I neared those
burial grounds. No matter how much I pretended I
wasn't scared, that made little difference in the way

I really felt! At evening time, when I would be walking back home, the eerie shadows of the tombstones would cause my imagination to run wild. There were times when I found myself running from my own shadow. How foolish all this sounds to me now! Yet those early childhood experiences are much like life itself: Even now there are moments when I catch myself running from the illusions of life, dreading those things that never happen, avoiding situations that are only frightening shadows of what might occur.

There is in all of us some "thing" which could give us a seizure of fear. Either that thing (or object or person) will control us or we will control it. So long as there have been people, these kinds of problems have existed. Family stress, sibling rivalry, murder, financial losses, sickness, and all the other things that touch us today are common to all of humankind. From the account of Cain, who slew his brother Abel, we see this shown in Adam and Eve's offspring. None of us is immune from difficulty or the unexpected factors which produce fear. In fact, most of our fears develop around the area of those uncertainties.

Someone once said, "Most of our vocational and lifethreatening situations occur within a span of two to three months. Since these changes come at unpredictable moments, we are usually unprepared to cope with them." Knowing the impossibility of foretelling our futures has caused us to lapse into a negative frame of mind, one that says, "No news is good news." Because fear comes in many different forms, we don't know how to deal with it, so we often label it in some cute psychological package and hope it will go away. These apprehensions are often long-standing and prohibit us from living freely. They cause us to become fearful in answering the phone because we are afraid of hearing a disconcerting message. Phobic reactions begin to take hold of us, keeping us bound in their viselike grip. Some of us have such deep-seated fears that we remain in our homes for years, unable to function in a gregarian society. Others of us will not ride airplanes, walk under ladders, step on cracks, or save a broken mirror. We are often held in bondage by these phobic superstitions.

The apostle Paul spoke to the young man Timothy, warning him about letting fear control him. It appears, from reading the account, that Timothy was having a problem in this area, and that the apostle wished to settle the issue at an early stage of his spiritual son's ministry. Not wanting to be offensive, but seeking to be firm, he must have pondered his words carefully. Can't you just imagine the learned apostle approaching this subject with his undergraduate ministerial student? First Paul reminds the young preacher of his early training, the qualities found in his mother and grandmother, and asks him to remember the gift that God had given earlier. Then he affirms Timothy by saying:

> God hath not given us the spirit of fear, but of power, and of love, and of a sound mind (2 Timothy 1:7 KJV).

If anyone in the world had a right to be fearful, Paul did! Look at him—shipwrecked, beaten, incarcerated, held captive by Roman soldiers. Still, he was the same man who reminded his follower, "God does not give us a spirit of fear." How could he be so positive in his statement on this subject?

The apostle Paul was speaking out of experience. He knew that if young Timothy was to be effective in ministry, he needed to learn well the lesson of courage. Paul described the condition of fear as being a "spirit of fear." Paul understood the importance of not permitting this dreaded attitude to become engrained in the youthful minister's thinking, for, should Timothy have allowed it, his life and ministry would soon have been adjusted to accommodate the fear syndrome.

When Fear Dominates

When fear dominates, it becomes both oppressive and possessive by nature. It is oppressive because our inner spirits are never free and possessive because it holds us within its grasp. Once we become victims to this dominating influence we are like a violin string stretched for performance. The string, when stretched too far, will eventually break. The instrument must be tuned with each corded thread in balance with the others in order to produce a harmonic sound. Life is no different: If fear stretches us too far, we are headed for breakage. Our lives are in discord when we begin to react in the following negative manner.

We equate God as being a hard taskmaster. Somehow we cannot perceive Him as being the loving Father that He is. The normal reactive covering is to feel that He is angry with us most of the time.

Not only so, but finding God's will becomes an arduous and burdensome task. The reason: We don't trust ourselves, and are bound by fear of doing the wrong thing. This indecisiveness on our part leads us to a state of ambivalence, and we begin to question God's leadership from the point of our own timidity.

When fear dominates, our fears run wild! Just as in my childhood days I could not discern the difference between the real and the imaginary, so fear often blinds us to the actual benefits of life. Or we may become so caught up in our compulsive thoughts that a protective rationalization process evolves. We think, *Why would this be happening to me? I am not worthy of God's blessings. Life is too complicated— there are too many unanswered questions. I am too confused to face life.* The imagination of our thoughts becomes compulsive behavioral patterns guiding us through life. It was for this very reason that the apostle Paul spoke to young Timothy as he did. What better person than Paul to deal with this? His words are just as encouraging to us today as he tells us how to cope with the mind-boggling question of fear:

> I use God's mighty weapons, not those made by man, to knock down the devil's strongholds. These weapons can break down every proud argument against God and every wall that can be built to keep men from finding Him (2 Corinthians 10:4,5).

Something else occurs when fear dominates: Because we are frightfully unsure of ourselves, we begin to feel the same way about other people as well. Everyone around us soon becomes suspect to our fears. The boss doesn't like us, the teacher is out to get us, our relatives don't care, and our spouses are not sensitive to our needs. These reactive coverings tend to wrap us up, holding us in and molding our thoughts into a hardened shell. If we do not recognize the problem for what it is, we will soon discredit those who love us most.

Our Provision

There is a way in which God has provided us a release from the poisonous "spirit of fear." We first learn to cope with it by learning what the antidote is. The solution to our problem is found in the word L-O-V-E! We cannot love God unless we make friends with Him, and permit Him to become our friend. J.I. Packer, in his book *Knowing God*, talks about how we imagine Him as being a glorified image of ourselves—just as weak as we are and having the same kinds of attitudes. Packer expresses such a deeply probing approach to knowing God that one could not read his book without a better understanding of how our fears are lost in the knowledge of who the heavenly Father is.

At this point we should rethink John 3:16: "Because God loved He gave—gave us His Son." Through a better and clearer understanding of that love, our fears will be assuaged—if we can apply the restorative balm that brings healing.

Place eight cards on a table. Label the first four cards F-E-A-R and the others L-O-V-E. Now place the cards reading "love" on top of those which say "fear." You can readily see that one cancels out the other.

F-E-A-R   L-O-V-E
(fear cancels love)   (love cancels fear)

God's love for us, and our being able to understand the meaning of that love, provides an antidote for our fears. Within the strength of knowing this love we accept God's willingness to give freely of His best. "God so loved the world that He gave . . ." (John 3:16).

The lavishness of His gift must be both recognized and accepted. The true earmark of a woman's freedom is seen in her ability to give, and to accept what is given. By receiving the free gift of Christ's love she incorporates the liberality of His Person into her daily thought processes. This opens her up and pulls her into harmony with life, allowing her pent-up fears to rest upon the caring nature of God.

Modern thought teaches us that, through a form of emotional release, we should displace our aggressive fears. We are encouraged to act out our hostile feelings against a person or object. However, we need only look at the biblical method to understand the difference between displacement and replacement. As Christians we don't just reshuffle our fears, hostilities, and anger; they are replaced with faith, hope, and trust in a God who helps us overcome them.

When Paul wrote his letter to the New Testament church in Philippi, he dealt with this problem of the mind. His words to the early church are just as relevant today as then. The apostle gave a method by which we can deal with our fear thoughts:

> Fix your thoughts on what is true and good and right. Think about things that are pure and lovely, and dwell on the fine, good things in others. Think about all you can praise God for and be glad about. Keep putting into practice all you learned (Philippians 4:8,9).

Can you face up to your problem with honesty? Is there a threatening situation in your life? If so, label it, confess it, and take possession of it.

1. Label your fears for what they really are, as opposed to what you may be tempted to think they are.
2. Confess them to God, asking His help in overcoming them.
3. Possess your fears by taking control of your life. Never permit fear to possess or control you.

Even after taking these steps, you may not be able to make a quick turnaround from your previous thought patterns. Don't give up—keep on trying. Hang onto the knowledge of God's ability to help you, and believe that He will. Once you have begun taking control of your reasoning powers by bringing God into focus for your needs, you are well on your way toward spiritual freedom. You see, it is not easy to face up to oneself! We are so tempted to hide behind facades, not wanting to call fear what it is: PRIDE! Fear becomes a form of pride when we resent knowing we cannot personally control everything that comes our way. Yet there are some things that we are unable to handle through our intellectual reasonings and brute strength. These things we must give to God, asking Him to help us toward human flexibility.

We all know that into each life a little tension must come. It is through this stress that our energy level rises, enabling us to defend ourselves. How we are able to cope with fear is determined largely by our ability to adapt.

When our two daughters were small I made most of their clothes. On my sewing machine was a tension knob, and while making a garment there were two things I needed to remember: Before being able to provide a good stitch, the thread had to be wrapped into the tension mechanism. This provided the "pull" necessary to give the fabric a tight seam. The other necessity was to make sure the knob was adjusted to fit the fabric with which I was working. If it was too tight, the seam puckered; too loose, and the stitches would not hold.

God works much the same way as He feeds the threads of life through His hand. Sometimes He tightens the tension to fit the fabric of our personalities; at other times the hold is loosened. When we attempt to adjust the threads to suit us, it just doesn't work — the seams holding us together will give way under the strain of daily living.

Our Promise

Do we have any promise that God's principles will work? There is an affirmative "yes" to that question. God's promises are sure, workable, and meant to help us! There is a clear statement of that truth in 1 John 4:18:

> We need have no fear of someone who loves us perfectly; his perfect love for us eliminates all dread of what he might do to us. If we are afraid, it is for fear of what he might do to us, and shows that we are not fully convinced that he really loves us. So you see, our love for him comes as a result of his loving us first.

The King James Version sums up these words by simply stating, "Perfect love casteth out all fear." The key word here is *perfect*. What is that perfection, and how do we become perfect in love? Does God demand human perfection of us before helping us? No! The meaning of the word "perfect," as written here, denotes a growing process. We can reach up to God out of the incompleteness of our growing knowledge, believing the action to be complete in His perfection. We don't need to be flawless—just perfectly willing to accept His infallibility.

Spiritual and psychological freedom is found in understanding the futility of our own efforts to manipulate our lives. Once we acknowledge that fact, we release God to work in our behalf, and He will set us free from the unsurmountable fear that may be holding us in bondage. You may be there right now, caught in the grasp of a life-threatening situation. Like a vise around your neck, it has a stranglehold on your inner psyche, and you feel stifled by its tightening grip. If so, draw strength from the psalmist, who was once where you now are. He prayed:

> When my heart is faint and over-whelmed, lead me to the mighty, tower-ing Rock of safety. For you are my refuge (Psalm 61:2,3).

One Bible commentator gave the precise transla-tion of the verse as being, "When the rock is too high for me, you take my hand and lead me." I like that because sometimes the mountain of fear is too high for us to surmount. When this is your plight, and you have done all that is humanly possible to climb over, ask God to lead you to the top, and He will!

Our youngest daughter, Jan, tells of her greatest moment of fear. She was diagnosed as being in the first stages of cancer. Caught in the grip of her fears, alone at night, apprehensive over surgery and the possibility of chemotherapy and radium treatments, she was overwhelmed with fright. There, in the blackness of the night, held sway by the denseness of her dreaded apprehension, she sought God's help. With one hand she turned on the bedside lamp, and with the other she reached for a book lying on the nightstand. Turning to Psalm 139 she began to read:

> 0 God, you know me inside and out,
>   through and through.
> Everything I do,
>   every thought that flits
>   through my mind,
>   every step I take,
>   every plan I make,
>   every word I speak,
> You know, even before these things
> happen.
>   You know my past;
>   You know my future.
>   —*Psalms Now*

She says that out of those words peace broke forth as she realized that God was in control of her situation. Prior to that time, she openly confesses, her life was quite predictable:

> There were only a few things in my life that I could not somehow manage. I was always a hardworking, and rather independent person. My self-sufficiency gave me a sense of personal security. But none of my ability mattered when the doctors gave me the medical report. I knew that

this was something over which I had
absolutely no control. That meant I would
have to trust myself into God's hand.

The rock that Jan was asked to climb was much
too high for her. It was one bigger than her self-
independence and personal ability to surmount. Yet
through it all she knew the Person of the Rock, Christ
Jesus. (Since her surgery she has been given a clean
bill of health. The doctor tells us that her condition was so minimal that it is of no future conse-
quence.) You may be right where she was, at a point
of desperation, viewing the jagged, cutting edges of
your fears. If so, look up, far above the mountains'
crevices. Somewhere in the distance is a hand reaching down to you. Take it and hold onto it, because
it is God's hand. He wants to carry you over your
mountain of fear!

Point of Action

1. Deliver your fears to God. Wrap them in a bundle
   of hope and lay them out in prayer.

2. Ask yourself what is meant by the "spirit of fear"
   as found in 2 Timothy 1:7 (KJV).

3. Listen with expectancy to what God wants to say
   to you.

4. List the fears that most trouble you.

5. Divide them:

Things I can help: Things I can't help:

Put the ones you can help on a separate piece of paper.

A. Pray about these fears every day as you seek God's help in overcoming them.
B. Be honest in your feelings as you express yourself to God.
C. Ask the Lord to give you insight as to why you are so fearful in these areas of life.
D. Be careful that you don't surround yourself with other fear-oriented persons.

Read Isaiah 41:10, Psalms 85 and 61.

THOSE WHO SEEK FREEDOM FIND IT NOT
ONLY FOR THEMSELVES BUT FOR OTHERS AS
WELL.

Chapter 13

Your Rewarding Search

Any woman who directs her search for freedom
in the path of God's providential guidance is sure to
find both help for her problems and strength to
surmount them.

Strength is provided as we allow God to become
a part of our struggle. Because He fully understands
us, He invites us to come to Him, come with our
burdens, the weariness we feel, our broken spirits,
and life's discontentment. When we accept His
invitation to come take His yoke, our burden then
becomes God's. The Lord entwines Himself with us,
becoming the equalizer or balancer of our lives.

No greater freedom will ever be known than that
which is realized through Jesus Christ. Whether our

needs are physical, psychological, emotional, or spiritual, they come to rest when given to Him. This is not meant to infer the need is no longer there, or that there is no need for effort on our part for meeting it. However, it does indicate a change on our part, a shift from our own self-efforts to a position of relaxed trust. The fact of knowing our goals are being pursued in step with His "yokemanship" keeps us in balance. Not only so, it relieves us from the urgency of that need. We, in turn, no longer feel captive or held back from the freedom we seek.

The Rewards of Seeking

Seeking freedom through a relationship with Jesus Christ provides us with an ongoing personal release toward growth. "Like a lamp to our feet," God's promises are enlightenment to our pathway. His slow, but certain light leads us one step at a time. There is no question, no point of argument on this matter. We know: "Those who seek do find" (Luke 11:9).

What is found? There are five elements of reward that are found in coming to Jesus Christ:

1. Time becomes our friend.
2. We learn, through the Lord, to make friends with ourselves.
3. We discover new freedoms and new avenues of expression.
4. We find the Lord at the pivotal point of our need.
5. Help will come to us through others and in the least expected way.

The reality of this last principle was made clear to

me recently as I lay on a hospital bed searching for answers to my own illness.

Donna and her husband, Len, had entered my room and were seated to the left of my bed. The August sun was beating hard against their backs as it shone through the patio window. Donna's dark hair was picking up the sunlight as it danced across her head. Like a crystal prism reflecting itself in mirrored glass, Donna's countenance was glowing in the sunlight.

How can this be? I wondered. *Why would they drive for almost an hour through the desert heat to visit me?* I had met them only briefly prior to this time. When Donna and her husband walked into my room where I was recuperating from a blood clot in my left lung, I knew their visit was for a purpose. Too weak to carry on an extended conversation, I could only listen. I did listen closely as Donna talked with me about her search for spiritual freedom:

> My life's goals were wrapped up in my vocational skills. As a critical care nurse in a nearby hospital, I had established a kind of personal independence. My peers had grown to respect me as a conscientious, well-trained worker, but they didn't know the battle that raged within me.
>
> My mother was a Christian woman, but some other members of my family were deeply rooted in witchcraft, Satanism, and the voodoo religion. The earliest memories I have are those of fear as relatives talked about putting "hexes" on people and pronouncing curses upon me. I grew into adulthood being tormented by the psychological and spiritual upheaval that was mounting

inside me. I felt myself in bondage to the threats and fears being imposed upon me by family members.

After my marriage to Len, whose family background was deeply steeped in the occult, I came to a breaking point. One day I found myself parked in the car on a lonely street in one of our California cities. Sitting there screaming out to God, I yelled:

"God, do You exist? If You do live and are real, will You please break away this bondage and set my spirit free?"

Then, an awakening came to me! Until that day there had been no release from my mental anguish. Something happened to me! For the first time in my long years of searching, help came. Once I called out to God, I sensed His presence. No, I didn't fully understand the enlightenment of the moment, but the slow, progressive steps toward freedom were becoming clearer.

A few days later, through a chain of unusual circumstances, I found my way to the home of a relative whom I had not seen for years. She introduced me to Christ who offered me the freedom I was seeking. I was set free! My soul, my spirit, were no longer captive in Satan's chains of bondage. The mental hold of psychological tyranny was severed. I was free from the hounding dread of a relative's wicked curse. Witchcraft and Satanism no longer controlled the behavioral patterns of my life. Voodooism, that had dogged my footsteps like a lioness seeking her prey, had become captive. . . instead of the captor. Embodied within Christ's invitation to "come" was the freedom I found as I became yoked with His love, peace, understanding, and forgiveness.

While Donna sat speaking about her search for freedom, I lay there bound by the physical weakness and bondage I felt. Not until that moment did I *fully* understand the depth of her freedom.

When Donna stood up from her chair, approached my bed, laid her hands on my head, and began praying for me, I knew how complete her freedom really was. She was free enough to move away from her self-needs to seek freedom for someone else . . . ME!

We are never more free than when we are free from self; so free we can become involved in seeking freedom for others, as well.

COME
(Matthew 11:28)

Come in your searching
and that search seems in vain.

Come with your sickness
and no rest from your pain.

Come with your sorrows
when tears abound.

Come with your disappointments
and there's no friend to be found.

Come with your weariness
when your strength is all gone.

Come with your hurting
and life has no song.

Come in the morning
of day's early dawn.

Come while the noonday
  lingers on.

Come in the evening
  of a long dreary day.

Come in the nighttime
  when sleep flies away.

Come into my rest,
  my healing,
    my strength.

For, in coming,
  you find
    the freedom
    you seek.

—Ruthe White